# Sculpture in Plastics

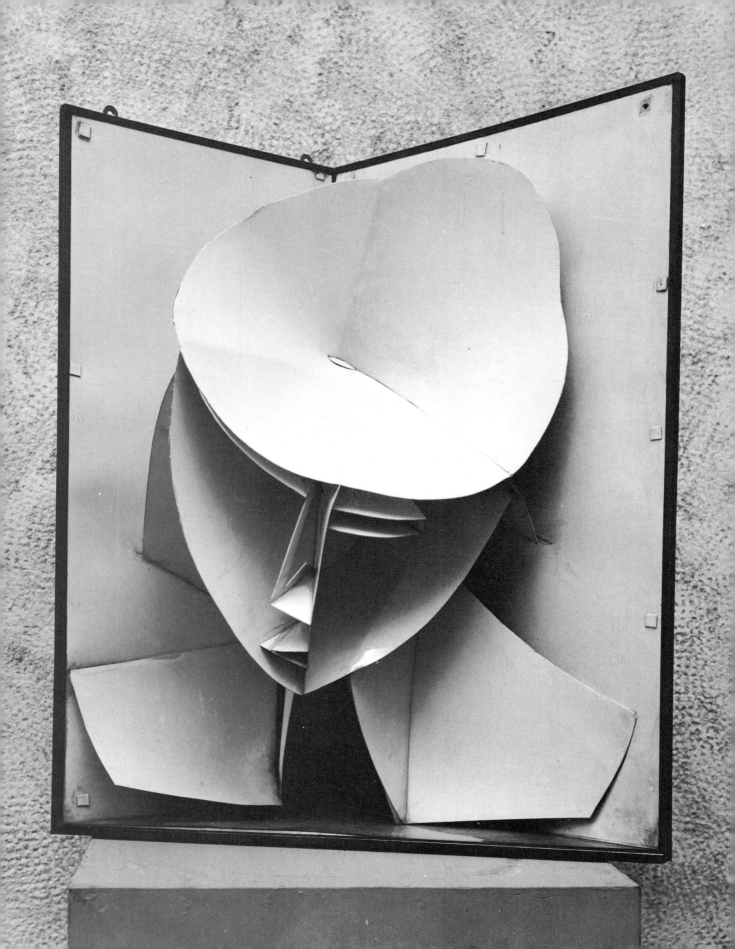

# Sculpture in Plastics

## BY NICHOLAS ROUKES

**WATSON-GUPTILL PUBLICATIONS** □ **NEW YORK**

**Head of a Woman** (1917-20) by Naum Gabo, 24½″ x 19¼″, celluloid and metal, Museum of Modern Art, New York.

*To Michael*

# Acknowledgments

The author is grateful to Dr. Rodney Roche of the Polymer Chemistry Laboratory of the University of Calgary, Alberta, for reading the manuscript and making technical suggestions; to Jonathan Batchelor, Robert Howard, St. Maur, Claude Blin, and Albert Vrana, for their contributions to the demonstration chapters; to the artists contributing photographs of their work for this publication; to James E. Simpson of the Ferro Corporation; to Trevor Long of the Royal College of Art, London; and to Neil Crichton for assistance in photography.

Special thanks to the many plastics manufacturers and distributors for technical information; to the Museum of Modern Art and the Whitney Museum, New York; to George Braziller, Inc.; to Donald Holden, the head-patting, Serbo-Croatian translator-editor at Watson-Guptill Publications; and to Glenna Roukes, without whom, etc., etc.

*Science and art, we are beginning to realize, are complementary forces, the yin and yang of the human spirit. . . . Science interprets the phenomenal world with reference to the coherences of structure and behavior. Art transforms the phenomenal world into poetic metaphors with reference to experiences unique to man.*

JULES LANGSNER
*Craft Horizons, January-February 1963*

# Contents

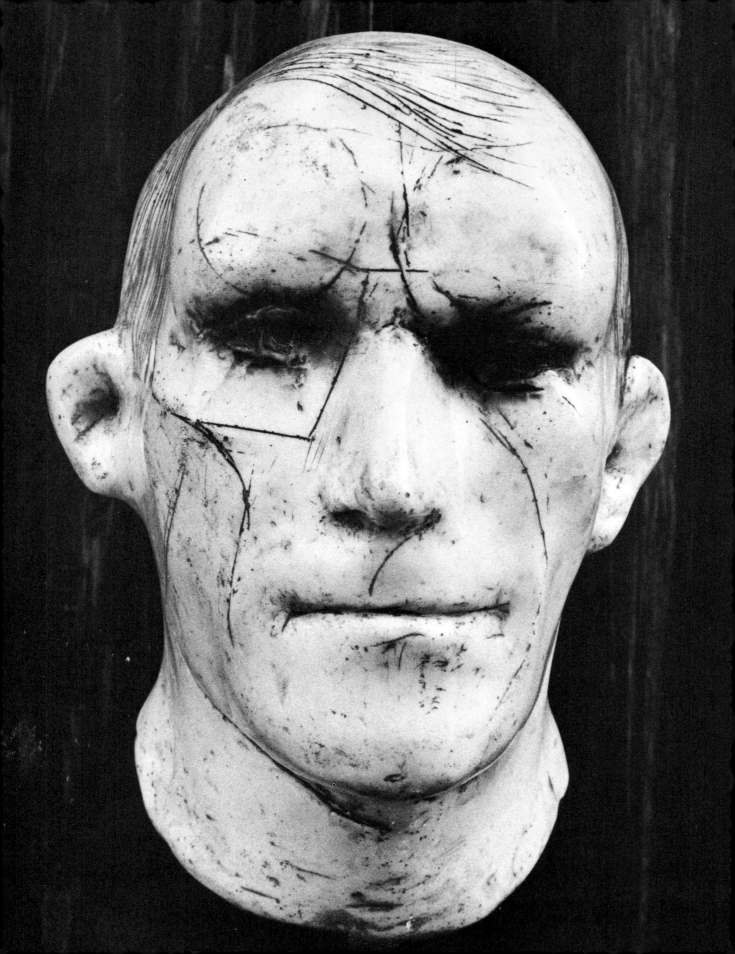

# Introduction

*It seems that art today, like a man, walks on two feet, a left foot that conquers, a right foot that holds. They complement, rather than contradict each other.* Michel Seuphor, THE SCULPTURE OF THIS CENTURY

Art, like man, passes through many epochs and cultures. Art identifies each age, as it affects and is affected by the age. In today's space age, art finds itself in a cosmos of remarkable technological advances.

From our scientific research laboratories, new galaxies of materials have been created — and continue to be created — which should stimulate and inspire the imagination of the artist.

As art walks on in search of new ideas, new concepts, and new materials, a right foot holds to the rich heritage of the past, while the left foot conquers in the search for contemporary methods and materials. Both complement one another as art searches for its identity in the twentieth century.

**Synthetic Materials**

It takes only a superficial glance at our surroundings to realize that many contemporary man-made objects are created of synthetic materials — which we call plastics. It is not only impossible to ignore the impact of the plastics industry; it is difficult to imagine living in this age without this industry's products. Already a billion dollar business, it continues to grow as it serves our present needs and as it plans for our life of tomorrow.

We find plastics used in cushions and chairs, floor coverings, wall tiles, lighting fixtures, and luggage. We sit in furniture made of plastic, wear plastic clothing, listen to music from plastic discs and tapes. We find plastic in photographic film, food wrappers, toys, signs, sporting equipment, packages, containers, and automobile bodies. Our own bodies are sometimes repaired surgically with life-giving plastic elements. Modern space vehicles and electronic computers utilize components of plastic. Even our credit cards are made of plastic.

When we look closely at the objects of our environment, it is apparent that literally thousands upon thousands of objects and machines which affect our daily lives are made of synthetic materials.

Less than one hundred years ago, these products did not exist. In this century, through creative chemistry, the scientist has combined oxygen,

**Head of Fighter** by Frank Gallo, 14″ x 10″ x 12″, epoxy, courtesy Graham Gallery, New York. This sculptor models in clay, casts in epoxy, then textures and colors the plastic with subtle, earthy colors.

hydrogen, nitrogen, chlorine, and sulphur to produce plastic materials unimaginable a few decades ago.

In the face of this remarkable creative activity among scientists, it is paradoxical to note that the artist has been lethargic to exploit these new materials which offer so many opportunities for creative expression. Held back, perhaps, by stereotyped notions, by ignorance, or by fear of new materials, he has penalized himself by failing to apply these challenging materials to fine art. There have been notable exceptions, however, and the list of those turning to synthetic materials is growing in number every year.

Marshall McLuhan poignantly focuses our attention on factors which have changed our lives in this electronic and polymer age. "Art has become co-extensive with discovery and knowledge in every sphere of action and at every possible stage of human development. The gap between art and technology has now ceased to exist. As we become cognizant of our art and technology as extensions of ourselves, we have also acquired the responsibility of heeding the psychic and social consequences of such extensions."

Artists of this century, witnessing an explosive expansion of human thought and experience, require radically new media capable of expressing the vital concepts which reflect the qualities of the life of this generation. Plastics are among the most exciting of these new media.

## A Radical Change in Sculpture

*"We affirm that the tone of a substance, i.e., its light-absorbing body, is its only pictorial reality."*

A sensation was created in art circles in the early 1920's by two brothers, Antoine Pevsner and Naum Gabo, who revolutionized sculpture by publishing a document entitled, *The Realist Manifesto.* This paper (quoted above) not only changed the direction of sculpture, but the impact of this manifesto still influences sculptors throughout the world.

In essence, the manifesto proclaimed that contemporary sculpture should unshackle itself from the heavy, monumental, and compact forms typical of the antecedent ages. The brothers' new concept of sculpture involved light, airy, transparent volumes. In many cases, their work emphasized transparent interpenetrations of form and space, often using a new plastic material — celluloid. They constructed their sculptures in an additive manner, emphasizing hollows and voids, and regarded sculpture as an expression of outward thrust. They became known as "constructivists," and led this important movement in art history.

Later, Pevsner worked with metal and turned to the use of the blowtorch as an art tool, while his brother, Gabo, pursued experiments with the new synthetic media, including the acrylic plastics. With his acrylic constructions, Gabo achieved classic contemporary forms, bringing a new reality to non-objective constructions with plastic and nylon cord. In 1942, he created *Linear Construction,* a work of acrylic and nylon. This work identified a new breed of artist, one who fused synthetic materials and modern concepts of form and space to produce an art form which was to mark a turning point in the art world.

Another pioneer in the use of plastics was Laszlo Moholy-Nagy, one of the original leaders of the Bauhaus school in the Germany of the 1920's. In the 1930's, Moholy-Nagy worked almost exclusively with Plexiglas acrylic sheets, which he heated and formed into multi-dimensional shapes, creating his renowned *Space Modulators*. In 1938, he moved to Chicago to found the new Bauhaus in America. His influence was widespread, and prior to his death in 1947, he made the following statement, which expressed his commitment to a new vision:

> *It is the artist's duty today to penetrate yet-unseen ranges of biological functions, to search the new dimensions of the industrial society and to translate the new findings into emotional orientation.*

The contemporary American sculptor Leo Amino was one of the first to use plastic for casting. His transparent sculpture, *The Family*, executed in 1948, involved the use of plastic resin with internal inclusions of color.

**A Sampling of the Possibilities**

Currently, there are a great number of sculptors using plastics in many ways. Franta Belsky, a British artist, uses polyester resin, mixed with metallic granules, in a system which he calls "cold metal casting." In the United States, Fred Dreher shapes solid acrylic blocks to create transparent sculpture which often features light sources in the base of the sculpture. Robert Mallary of New York dips fabrics and "ready-founds" into catalyzed liquid polyester, then arranges the shapes which the plastic has transformed from flexible materials into rigid, three-dimensional sculpture. Domenico Mortellito carves rigid foamed plastic to produce large, lightweight sculpture. Freda Koblick of San Francisco pours acrylic monomer to create prism shapes which she utilizes in making constructions and lighting fixtures. French artist, Kosice, creates hollow, liquid-filled forms of acrylic plastic, which he later uses for his "hydro-mobiles." Claes Oldenberg of New York has created "soft sculpture," using various types of vinyl and cellular plastics. Contemporary sculptors, of course, have found a motherlode of plastic materials for various types of kinetic sculptures.

These, obviously, are some of the more unusual uses of plastics in sculpture, mentioned only to show that this is a multi-purpose material, which can be used in an immense variety of ways. In the chapters to follow, I will discuss some of my own experiments, and those of sculptors whom I have met in the United States and abroad.

Overly technical terms, charts, and complex chemical formulae will be avoided in this book. As an artist speaking to other artists, art students, art educators, and Sunday sculptors, I will seek to describe the plastics field in understandable, practical terms which the reader can put to immediate and productive use.

**Linear Construction in Space, No. 4** (left) (1958) by Naum Gabo, 40″ x 21½″, plastic and stainless steel, Whitney Museum of American Art, New York. The complex planes of this intricate work are all woven of plastic fibers.

**Double Loop** (below left) (1946) by Laszlo Moholy-Nagy, 24″ long, acrylic, Museum of Modern Art, New York. A single sheet of Plexiglas was cut, shaped, and curved to produce an intricate interplay of linear edges and transparent planes.

**Torso** (right) (1924-26) by Antoine Pevsner, 29½″ high, plastic and copper, Museum of Modern Art, New York, Katherine S. Dreier bequest. In this pioneer work, the sculptor has curved and bolted together sheets of plastic and copper.

**Bust** (below right) by Antoine Pevsner, 20⅞″ x 23⅜″, celluloid and metal, Museum of Modern Art, New York. This early exploration of the possibilities of opaque, transparent, and perforated forms was done in 1923-24.

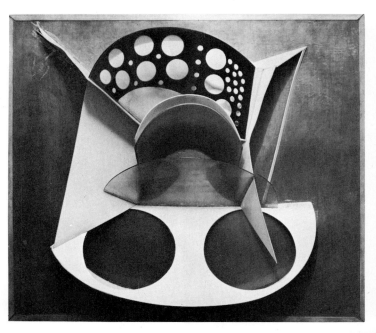

**Transformation Instable 27** by Francisco Sobrino, 80 x 80 x 27 cm., toned transparent acrylic sheet. Although sculptural in construction, Sobrino's work creates an ambiguous space through the use of transparent materials, cut and intricately assembled. Spectator movement creates new relationships of shapes and colors.

# Plastics for Sculpture 1

The ubiquitous term, *plastic*, is indeed ambiguous in its meaning. *Plastic* actually describes a *property* or *properties* displayed by a particular material. In its literal, dictionary sense, a material is *plastic* if it has been — or can be — altered by the use of external force, heat, or pressure. The term further denotes that the altered material has also *maintained* its new shape or form. Thus, by this definition, we can see that a great number of materials are plastic in that they display plastic characteristics.

Clay, for example, is a *natural* plastic material, which may be shaped, fired, and thus changed into many rigid forms. Rubber, wax, and shellac are other such natural materials.

When early *synthetic* substances also displayed these mentioned properties, they too were promptly dubbed *plastic*, a term which stuck. However, just as we define the various types of metals — such as aluminum, brass, and copper — within broader categories of metals, plastics are also defined according to their specific type: phenolics, polyesters, epoxies, acrylics, etc. For the purposes of the sculptor, there are two basic groups of plastics: thermoplastic and thermosetting.

*Thermoplastic resins* are plastics which become soft when they are exposed to sufficient heat and which harden when cool. They will do this no matter how many times the process of heating and cooling is repeated. This group of plastics includes the acrylics, cellulosics, nylon, polyethylene, polystyrene, polyfluorocarbons, vinyls, polyvinylidene, ABS, acetal resin, polypropylene, and polycarbonates.

**Two Basic Groups of Plastics**

*Thermosetting plastics* achieve their final shape when heat *and* pressure are applied to them during their forming process. Reheating does *not* soften these plastics. This group includes the phenolics, amino plastics, polyesters, epoxies, silicones, alkyds, allylics, and caseins.

Synthetic resin constitutes the basic ingredient of plastics. This is an organic substance made synthetically by the process of polymerization. Many ingredients are added to the resin, such as fillers, plasticizers, antioxidants, colorants, stabilizers, and catalysts. These elements control the eventual properties of the final plastic; thus, the manufacturer is able to tailor-make a variety of plastics to suit the demands of industry.

Plastics are manufactured in the form of liquids, pastes, pellets, powders, foams, emulsions, sheets, rods, tubes, and solid volumes. They may be used in a variety of ways: they may be cast, formed, molded, extruded, laminated, and fabricated.

In fine art, plastics are used either by themselves or in conjunction with other materials. In some instances — such as in some techniques using foamed plastics — they may be used as a temporary material, to be cast later in metal.

**Studio Practices Using Plastics**

Plastics respond readily to a variety of techniques and processes. Listed below are some that are used most frequently.

(1) *Laminating:* You can fabricate with liquid polyester and fibreglass cloth, or "sandwich" transparent materials within polyester resin.

(2) *Forming:* You can use plastic for cutting, heat bending, machining, bonding, and vacuum forming.

(3) *Casting:* You can cast liquid resins (such as polyesters, epoxies, and acrylic monomers) into molds or forms to create three-dimensional sculpture or panels.

(4) *Carving:* You can carve cellular plastics, solid acrylic blocks, or laminated volumes.

(5) *Impregnating:* You can use polyester resin to saturate loose materials or fabrics to create solid forms; sealing, coating, and painting operations will protect porous materials or improve surface characteristics.

(6) *Polychroming:* You can paint sculpture (natural or synthetic materials) with plastic based paints.

**Joining Plastics**

There are four basic methods of joining plastics: mechanical linkage, adhesive bonding, thermal bonding, and solvent bonding.

(1) *Mechanical linkage* methods involve the use of rivets, nuts and bolts, self-tapping metal screws, hinges, clips, etc. Metalworking or woodworking linkage devices are readily adapted to plastics.

(2) *Adhesive bonding* involves the use of adhesives which will bond plastics together without dissolving or otherwise damaging surfaces. The best bonding agents include the epoxy resin based adhesives.

(3) *Thermal bonding* of thermoplastics involves the use of heat, which softens plastic surfaces and effects a welded joint. Heated tools, high frequency electric devices, friction tools, and hot gas tools are commonly used for this type of bonding.

(4) *Solvent bonding* of thermoplastics is effected by using solvents which soften plastic surfaces and fuse plastics together. Acrylic plastics are usually solvent bonded by using ethylene dichloride, methylene dichloride, or methyl methacrylate monomer 40%. These solvents are applied by dropper, brush, hypodermic needle, glass tube or rod.

Accompanying the widespread growth of plastics, there has been an unfortunate proliferation of plastic material in poorly designed, mass-produced goods. Although there have been many excellent products designed in plastics, plastic may still signify inexpensive, production-line items to the average consumer. However, the discriminating consumer — and the sculptor who has looked beyond the "Donald Duck" debasement of some plastics — know that rich, honest means of expression are possible.

Plastics are a new sculptural medium which should be added to the list of materials for the artist's use, along with stone, metal, and wood. The artist should use plastics when he thinks he may use them *honestly,* that is, when they are able to do something which other materials cannot.

What, then, are some of the inherent qualities of the material and some of the honest uses of plastics? There are many types of plastics, of course, and each offers specific advantages. . . .

For example, some polyester casting resins, acrylic sheets, and monomers are transparent. Transparent sculpture is a fairly new concept in art, involving the idea of allowing light to *enter* a sculpture. Liquid transparent resins may also be cast with dyes or "inclusions."

Clear acrylic plastics have the uncommon ability to "pipe" light. Light is captured, flows through the material, and is refracted towards the edges. The edges, or incised carvings on the surface, seem to glow with unusual brilliance. A sculptor may use artificial light to control this characteristic.

Most plastics are essentially lightweight; therefore, large architectural works may be created in the artist's studio rather than at the site, and transportation costs are considerably lower than the cost of shipping stone or metal. Some of the lighter plastics — such as styrofoam or other foamed plastics — may be used as *molds* for concrete casting, or as a temporary material which will later be vaporized with hot metal for bronze casting.

Plastics are strong, durable, dimensionally stable, and easily formed without expensive machinery. Some plastics — such as the epoxies or isopthalic polyesters — will adhere to many materials. In putty form, plastics are ideal as a build-up medium: they can be used on forms or armatures of many dissimilar materials to yield strong, permanent sculptures. Because of the consistency of the putty plastics, inclusions (such as metallic granules, rocks, minerals, or other filler) may be added by the sculptor.

An innovation in lost wax casting involves plastics. Sculptures made of wax may be invested in plaster and the wax burned out. These hollow molds may then be used for casting with liquid plastic. The plaster may be broken away later to release the casting.

Thermoplastic materials (such as acrylic sheet) may be heated and formed into a variety of three-dimensional shapes, an uncommon advantage. Furthermore, these materials may be bonded together to form opaque or transparent architectural panels or three-dimensional sculpture.

As we begin to examine the nature of some of these plastics, a new world of possibilities begins to unfold.

**Hoboken #10** (above) by Roger Bolomey, 48″ x 56″, polyurethane, courtesy Royal S. Marks Gallery, New York. When he creates his cellular foam sculptures, this sculptor works in a specially made safety chamber, using liquid components for foamed plastics.

**Magiscopes** (right) by Feliciano Bejar, polyester, acrylic, and inclusions, courtesy Bertha Schaefer Gallery, New York. Glass, lenses, clockworks are bonded with polyester to clear acrylic sheet and fitted to metal forms. Lenses are ground of acrylic, producing varied illusions.

**String Composition #119** (above) by Sue Fuller. Collection, Mr. and Mrs. Joseph L. Braun. Photo courtesy Bertha Schaefer Gallery, New York. A labyrinth of woven saran plastic threads evolves a poetry of straight lines and curvilinear forms.

**3807-17** (left) by Norman Zammitt, 13″ high, acrylic, courtesy Felix Landau Gallery, Los Angeles. Transparent, colored acrylic sheet is cut and assembled with mathematical precision.

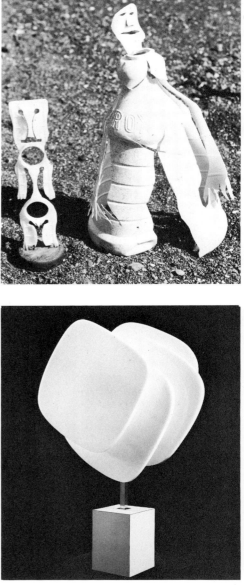

**Brave New World** (above left) by Nicholas Roukes, 48″ x 63″, polyurethane and mixed media. Carved forms of rigid polyurethane were coated with catalyzed thixotropic polyester resin. Aluminum wire and glass tesserae were also incorporated into this bas relief.

**Clorox and His Faithful Servant** (upper right) by Art Grant, vinyl. Plastic bottles and other "junk" are transformed by this sculptor into whimsical sculptural creations.

**CCR** (lower right) by Colin Greenly, 47″ x 31″, acrylic, courtesy Bertha Schaefer Gallery, New York. Opaque acrylic sheet was cut and assembled to produce an effect of great elegance and simplicity. Note the reflections of the sheets in one another.

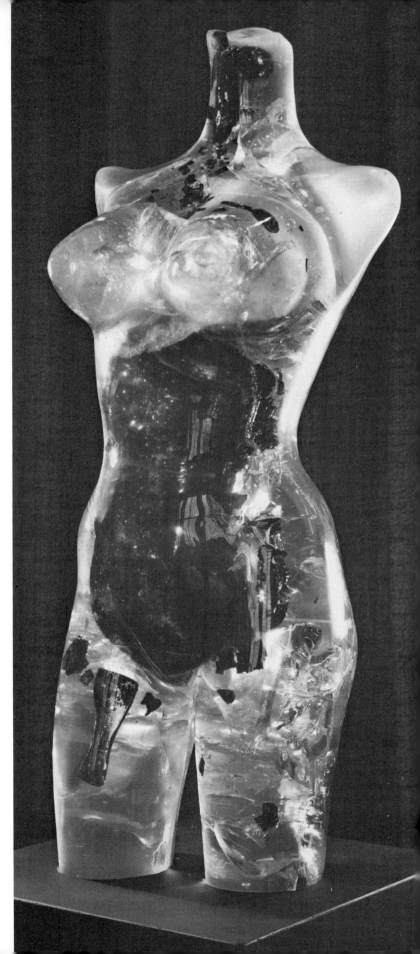

**Justine de Sade** by Arman, 35″ x 12″, polyester and embedded objects, courtesy Sidney Janis Gallery, New York. Objects were inserted in the mold and then the liquid polyester resin was poured over them.

# Polyester 2

Polyester resin is a liquid plastic material with a viscosity somewhat like syrup. It is described as a thermosetting, unsaturated alkyd resin which is dissolved in styrene and other monomers. Polyester requires the use of a catalyst which is added to the liquid resin, producing a chemical heat or exotherm that *cures* the resin, changing it from a liquid to a solid state. Now, what do these technical terms mean?

Because this material may be cured in normal room temperatures, it lends itself to many techniques and processes in sculpture. First of all, polyester is a *thermosetting* plastic; once it has hardened into a solid, it becomes a permanent, insoluble material. As a solid, it may be sanded, machined, drilled, or treated with a variety of shop tools.

**Characteristics of Polyester Resins**

To implement the curing of polyester resin, the sculptor needs only to add a catalyst (a chemical which sets the curing process in motion) in the proper proportion, which is determined by three factors: the thickness to be poured; atmospheric temperature which would affect the cure; and the *pot life* desired — that is, how long he wants the material to remain workable before it cures. Typical catalysts are chemicals such as benzoyl peroxide and methyl ethyl ketone peroxide.

Air inhibits the curing of polyester resins. Thus, special formulations are created for open lay-ups — laminations which must cure in open air, rather than in molds. These are generally called *surfacing resins.* They contain small amounts of paraffin wax, which rises to the surface to effect a surface seal and promote surface hardening.

Polyester resins display many desirable chemical qualities. They are flame-resistant and often self-extinguishing. They vary in color from pale straw to purple to completely clear. They resist temperatures up to approximately 250°F. (some up to 500°F.). They are chemically resistant to oils, dilute acids, and alkalis. And they exhibit excellent tensile strength, which may be increased about seven times when polyester is laminated with fibreglass.

Polyester resins are characterized by a distinct odor, which is inoffensive and disappears once the resin has hardened or *polymerized.* This resin has a shelf life of about one year when stored in a cool area (0-40°F.) or about six months when stored in normal room temperatures (about 70°F.). Curing is best effected at normal room temperatures (about 70°F.).

The adhesive qualities of polyester resins lend themselves to lay-up or lamination — in combination with fibreglass, for example. For the same reason, polyester resins are good binders for fillers such as metallic powders, crushed stone, and other organic or inorganic bodies for casting. The excellent clarity of the casting resins lends these materials splendidly to transparent sculpture techniques.

Because the syrupy resin has a tendency to run off vertical surfaces, manufacturers are now producing *thixotropic* polyester resins, which have a heavy, putty-like consistency. These resins contain thickeners which enable the polyester to hold to vertical surfaces; the thixotropic material can be applied in thick, pasty batches to molds. The sculptor may easily make his own thixotropic polyester resin by adding fillers which are described in this chapter.

**Properties of Polyester as a Sculpture Medium**

Particularly interesting to the sculptor are the following characteristics of polyester resins:

(1) *Lightweight:* These materials will yield sculptures which are much lighter than traditional materials such as metal or stone; this lightness facilitates the shipping and handling of large scale sculpture.

(2) *Strength:* The materials are inherently strong; some are as strong as metal. Fillers and fibreglass increase strength approximately seven times. The resins are weather and water resistant. The 7.5% linear shrinkage may be reduced by the use of fillers.

(3) *Ease of fabrication and handling:* Polyesters require no special tools in handling, and the sculptor may manage the entire phase of his work in his studio. Polyester may be sawed with common saws; drilled or sanded with hand or power equipment; buffed and polished easily to a high gloss.

**Uses of Polyester in Sculpture**

In addition to lamination with fibreglass, here are other significant uses.

(1) *Transparent casting:* Used with plaster molds or other types of molds, clear polyester resin will produce transparent sculpture which may or may not contain inclusions. Inclusions such as dyes, glass, semi-precious stones, or loose objects may become an internal part of the transparent casting. Inbedment or encapsulation of materials is easily achieved. Internal crackles of cast polyester forms may be controlled by gas vent manipulation.

(2) *Plastic-metal casting:* Using polyester resin with granules — such as sintered bronze powder — the sculptor may create "bronze" castings, called the *cold casting* method by many artists. Metallic powders of bronze, copper, aluminum, and other materials are successfully used in this method. Plastic-stone casting — whereby polyester resin is mixed with crushed marble, granite, or other such materials — will yield beautiful effects.

(3) *Impregnation:* The excellent penetrating characteristics of polyester resins make them outstanding as surfacing or coating mediums for porous materials such as masonry or wood. Burlap, canvas, and other fabrics — even leather — may be impregnated with polyester to produce rigid forms for sculpture.

(4) *Mold material for cement casting:* Fibreglass and polyester molds — taken from sculpture of plaster, cellular foam, or other materials — will yield a high strength mold, suitable for casting concrete architectural panels.

**Pot Life**

As soon as the sculptor adds the catalyst to the polyester resin, a definite working time period is immediately established; at the end of this period, the catalyzed resin will inevitably change into an infusible solid. The period during which this irreversible process takes place is referred to as the *pot life* of the catalyzed resin. Pot life will, of necessity, be an important consideration in dealing with this resin. As the resin hardens, there are three important time periods:

(1) *Gel time:* This marks the time during which the resin changes into its in-between state, that of a jelly-like substance.

(2) *Ready for sanding:* This is the time when the resin is hard enough to sand, yet not completely cured (about 24 hours).

(3) *Complete cure:* This means *complete* polymerization, which may take approximately a week, depending on the amount of catalyst used, climatic conditions, and temperature. At this time, the resin is fully cured and water will *not* cause the surface to whiten or *blush.*

**Curing Process**

As mentioned earlier, the polyester resins are thermosetting materials and require heat to harden or polymerize them. Even if left in a warm room or placed in an oven for a prolonged time, the resins would eventually harden by themselves. However, this process is hastened by the addition of a catalyst to the resin. When combined with the accelerator or "promoter" which is already within the resin (added by the manufacturer), the catalyst promotes an artificial or chemical heat, which hardens the resin in anywhere from five minutes to 10 hours, depending on the combinations used and climatic conditions.

This internal (or exothermic) heat is controlled by the addition of the proper amounts of catalyst. Too much heat can produce an excessive exothermic reaction which may cause cracks and fissures; not enough may present problems of improper hardening, resulting in tacky surfaces and poor mold release. In laminating or lay-up techniques, where large surface areas are open to the atmosphere, larger amounts of catalyst may be employed

**Kiss** (right) by Marisol, 9½″ x 8½″ x 6″, polyester, metal, and light, courtesy Sidney Janis Gallery, New York. The artist exploits the light conducting quality of the translucent material.

**Architectural Wall** (below) by William Mitchell, 270′ x 14′6″, polyester and fibreglass. Lucas Experimental Laboratories. This is a polyester and fibreglass lamination with glazes of colored polyester.

for faster curing. In this case, exothermic heat is readily dissipated into the atmosphere. But in casting compact, massive forms, smaller amounts of catalyst must be used because large surface areas — which dissipate heat — are not present, and the exothermic heat within the casting builds to a point where there may be cracking or fissuring. Peak exothermic heat is generally around 270°-285°F. Some resilient polyester resins build higher peak exotherms, approaching 450°F., while others have very low exothermic reactions, below 200°F.

The sculptor should consider carefully the type of polyester resin he requires: whether it is a laminating type, which usually calls for quicker curing and hotter exotherms; or whether it is a casting polyester resin, which is formulated for longer curing periods and lower exothermic heat reaction. Manufacturers indicate on the packages of their products the amount of catalyst to be used with the resin. When you use laminating resins, these directions should be followed carefully. However, experience has shown that very little catalyst is necessary in voluminous casting. It is wise to experiment by using very small amounts of catalyst in making volume castings; furthermore, you can dissipate exothermic heat by incorporating fillers in the resin.

**Catalysts**

Principal catalysts used with polyester resins are organic peroxides. Methyl ethyl ketone (MEK) peroxide is most frequently used. Although available in paste and powder forms as well, *liquid* catalyst is generally used. The sculptor should be extremely careful in handling this chemical, as it is toxic, flammable, and explosive if subjected to severe shock or decomposition. These chemicals contain large amounts of active oxygen.

Generally, the artist uses very small quantities of organic peroxides in the studio, and most of the types sold in art and boat shops are diluted to make them less sensitive to shock. However, it should be emphasized that a freshly poured casting of catalyzed resin should never be placed in an oven, as the violent decomposition of the catalyst may be explosive.

**Thinning Polyester Resin**

Although this is seldom necessary, polyester resins may be thinned with styrene monomer to facilitate the penetration of porous materials such as masonry or wood. Although the thinned resin offers deeper penetration, no more than 15% of the styrene monomer should be used. Using more than this tends to weaken the resin. Note that more catalyst is required when the resin is thinned because the curing time is prolonged.

Do *not* use acetone or lacquer thinners for thinning polyester resins; these chemicals are used only for cleanup purposes.

**Thickening Polyester Resin**

A variety of fillers may be mixed with the polyester resin to create thicker mixes. These mixtures may be applied to vertical surfaces in lay-up or casting,

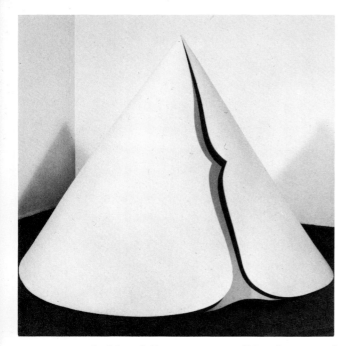

**Rosebud** by Phillip King, 60″ x 72″, polyester and fibreglass, courtesy Richard Feigen Gallery, New York. This four piece lamination uses wood for structural support.

**Structure** by St. Maur, 18″ high, polyester. This was a massive casting of thixotropic polyester into a prepared plaster mold. The resin contained integral color.

**Ellinikon** by Nicholas Roukes, approximately 16″ x 20″, polyester. Catalyzed polyester was cast directly into damp pottery clay, which had been depressed and textured with various tools. Acrylic paint washes were pooled on the surface.

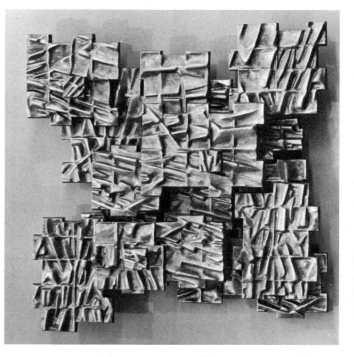

**Relief** by François Stahly, 12′ x 12′, polyester. This type of relief can either be built up directly by laminating polyester and fibreglass over precut forms, or it can be executed as a lay-up within a suitable mold.

and the fillers help to hold heavier particles — such as crushed stone or metallic powders — in proper suspension.

Generally speaking, up to 40% of filler may be added to the polyester resin without weakening it. In fact, these fillers *increase* the strength of the resin, control the exothermic reaction, effect opacity, reduce shrinkage, and improve the general appearance of the material. In addition, they appreciably cut the cost of working with polyester.

**Fillers for Polyester Resin**

Both organic and inorganic fillers may be used with polyester resins. Typical materials include: chopped or milled glass fibers, synthetic fiber, flock, asbestos fibers, silica, china clay, talc, chalk, pumice, sand, minerals, whiting, pearlite, gypsum, wood or shell flour, and sawdust. Colloidal silica, such as Cab-O-Sil, is often used in commercial thixotropic polyester pastes.

Microballoons — tiny, hollow spheres of Bakelite — may also be mixed with polyester resin to obtain a syntactic foam, a cellular plastic with an attractive surface texture.

**Pigments for Polyester Resins**

Pigments, especially prepared to color polyester resins, are available in paste, powder, or liquid form. Most boat or craft shops which carry the resin also carry these pigments. The experimental sculptor, however, will find a great number of ingredients that will work quite well in coloring polyester resins. Try experimenting with various types of dry colors, dyes, metallic powders, tinting pastes, and inks for a variety of colorful effects.

The coloring medium should be added to the resin *before* the catalyst is introduced, then thoroughly mixed. Since some dyes are extremely potent, only a few drops may be necessary. If succeeding, similar batches are to be mixed, careful notations should be made as to the amount of color used with each quantity of resin to insure uniform color.

Some of the colors may inhibit or accelerate the cure time slightly, and variations of the amount of catalyst may be required. Certain reds and yellows, for example, inhibit the cure of the resin, and larger amounts of catalyst are necessary. If you are doubtful about the nature and chemical effect of the color, it is wise to test first.

Adding color to the polyester resin produces *integral* color: the color is *in* the substance, not merely on the surface. Subsequent sanding or polishing; therefore, will not remove the color, as with surface coatings.

**Problems Often Encountered**

Here are some common problems that occur in using polyester resins — plus the most frequent causes and suggested remedies.

(1) *Cracks, fissures:* Too much catalyst used, or catalyst was too hot for particular resin. Cut down the amount of catalyst. Use a lower exo-

thermic reaction catalyst. Use fillers to absorb exothermic heat. Add up to 10% flexible resin.

(2) *Tacky surface, uneven curing:* Inadequate hardening is usually caused by the inhibiting air, insufficient or improperly mixed catalyst. Use more catalyst. Put cellophane over the surface to cut out air. Use surfacing resin. Stir the catalyst well into the resin.

(3) *Warping:* This is usually caused by high curing temperatures, or uneven mixing of the catalyst.

(4) *Bubbles:* Air has probably been whipped into the resin while adding and mixing the catalyst.

(5) *Whitening of surface (blushing):* Water or moisture has made contact with resin that has not completely polymerized. Delay wet sanding.

**Available Types of Commercial Polyester Resin**

In determining which type of polyester resin to use, the artist should first consider the type of sculpture he wishes to create, and should then determine the specific demands of the project.

Listed below are the various forms of commercially available polyester resins. These may be purchased at boat shops, hobby or craft shops, paint stores, and some art supply stores. Sources of supply are listed at the end of this book. Polyester resins are usually packaged in pints, quarts, gallons, and five gallon containers. The price usually includes the catalyst, which comes in a separate plastic bottle.

(1) *Surfacing polyester resins:* These resins are ideal for finish coats. They surface cure to a hard, dry surface. They contain wax, which rises to the surface during cure, creating a barrier to prohibit air from inhibiting the cure of the resin.

(2) *Bond coat polyester resin* does not surface cure: it remains tacky on the surface, making it ideal for fibreglass lamination. A final coat of surfacing resin is required to obtain the hard, dry surface of fibreglass sculpture. This resin *does* cure against a mold surface — that is, within a mold — or when plastic sheeting is pressed over the surface to keep the air away.

(3) *Thixotropic polyester resin:* These resins are basically the same as the surfacing resins, except that thixotropic resins have fillers incorporated to give them a slightly heavier body.

(4) *Thixotropic paste resin:* This is a polyester resin prepared in very thick paste form. The filler is usually a colloidal silica such as Cab-O-Sil. This paste can be dyed, pigmented, or used with metallic fillers or heavier bodied fillers. Paste polyester helps to keep in suspension the heavy particles which are mixed with it. The resin is mixed with the catalyst, and applied with a spatula to molds, etc. It is very good for the additive

**A** (left) by Derrick Woodham, 58″ x 63″ x 24″, painted polyester and fibreglass, courtesy Richard Feigen Gallery, New York. Laminations, done with care, can produce exceptional purity of form.

**Custodian** (below) by Robert Howard, 42″ x 63″ x 75″, cores of balsa wood were painted with polyester resin and wrapped with fibreglass tape in several laminations. The final surface texture was created by sifting fine redwood sawdust over wet catalyzed polyester resin. This stabile was made in four basic sections, calculated for slow, undulating movement.

sculpture process—building polyester directly over armatures and cores. This paste may also be spread evenly over a surface; various objects can then be pressed into the mix for assemblages or mosaics.

(5) *Clear polyester casting resins* are used for creating clear castings or transparent laminations. These resins may be used with dyes, other colorants, and inclusions such as glass, metal, etc.

(6) *Polyester (or epoxy) automobile body pastes:* These putties (available from automotive supply stores) are excellent for sculpture. They usually include an isophthalic resin, which produces a thick putty consistency with good flexibility. Mixed with hardener, the paste may be used to build directly over armatures of wire, screen, etc.

(7) *Isophthalic polyester resin* is a flexible polyester resin with inherent properties of adhesiveness and elasticity. It withstands the differential coefficients of thermal expansion of dissimilar laminated materials. Used primarily in lamination, it is tough, adhesive, and wax free. Laminations must be given a final coating of surfacing resin for a hard, dry surface. Isophthalic polyester resin is recommended for laminating or bonding dissimilar materials.

**General Precautions for Personal Safety**

Many of the basic materials, solvents, and thinners used for making sculpture from plastics may present health hazards if improperly used or handled. Strict safety precautions and hygienic procedures should be exercised at all times.

Liquids and vapors from such materials as acetone and styrene are flammable, explosive, and toxic. Catalysts are toxic and highly unstable materials. When subjected to heat or shock, these agents may produce a violent reaction. Vapors from most of these materials are to be avoided and adequate ventilation should be provided.

As most of these materials are toxic, the sculptor is urged to check the manufacturer's directions as to proper use, handling, and suggested safety precautions in using *any* plastic product or accessory material. The following safety precautions should be observed carefully:

(1) *Ventilation:* Always work in a properly ventilated studio. Avoid enclosed areas when working with polyesters and their companion chemicals. Fumes and vapors are toxic and should be avoided. When working with polyesters over a continuous period, have extractor fans and vent hoods installed to keep the air in the studio constantly fresh. Use disposable containers for mixing and use disposable plastic gloves to avoid skin contact with resins and chemicals.

(2) *Catalysts:* Catalysts for polyester are highly toxic, flammable, and explosive materials. They should be kept away from heat or flame and

protected from shocks or falls. Skin contact with these chemicals should be avoided. Some resins require a catalyst in a two-part system, involving a promoter plus the catalyst; if you are handling this type of resin, exercise due caution to keep the accelerator and catalyst separate. Never mix these two chemicals as they will rapidly decompose or explode. For safer handling, it is suggested that the sculptor use the *pre-accelerated* polyester resin (which already contains the accelerator), to which you add only the single chemical catalyst.

(3) *Glass cloth:* Remember that glass cloth is actual glass fiber from spun glass. When you use this material over a prolonged period wear protective gloves to avoid splinters.

(4) *Sanding polyester:* In sanding cured polyester, avoid breathing the dust. Wear protective goggles, a respirator mask, and protective clothing to prevent irritation to the eyes, skin, or respiratory tract from the dust. Wet sanding is recommended to alleviate dust conditions.

(5) *Acetone, lacquer thinners:* These thinners are generally used for cleanup of brushes, tools, etc. They are highly flammable, generally toxic and should be treated carefully. Acetone has a very low flash point and is extremely flammable. Avoid skin contact with acetone and be sure your work area is well ventilated.

Disposable paper should be used to protect work benches, and good housekeeping should be observed. Promptly dispose of contaminated papers, mixing cans, etc. *Do not smoke or eat* while using these chemicals. Careless contact with these chemicals may cause skin allergies, dermatitis, or toxic conditions of more serious consequence. Professional sculptors urge beginners to exercise extreme caution in handling the chemicals associated with polyester resins.

In the demonstration chapters which follow, four principal techniques, listed below, will be described: (1) laminating with fibreglass cloth; (2) casting with metallic fillers and other bodies; (3) transparent casting; (4) impregnating porous materials and polyester coatings.

**Methods of Working with Polyester**

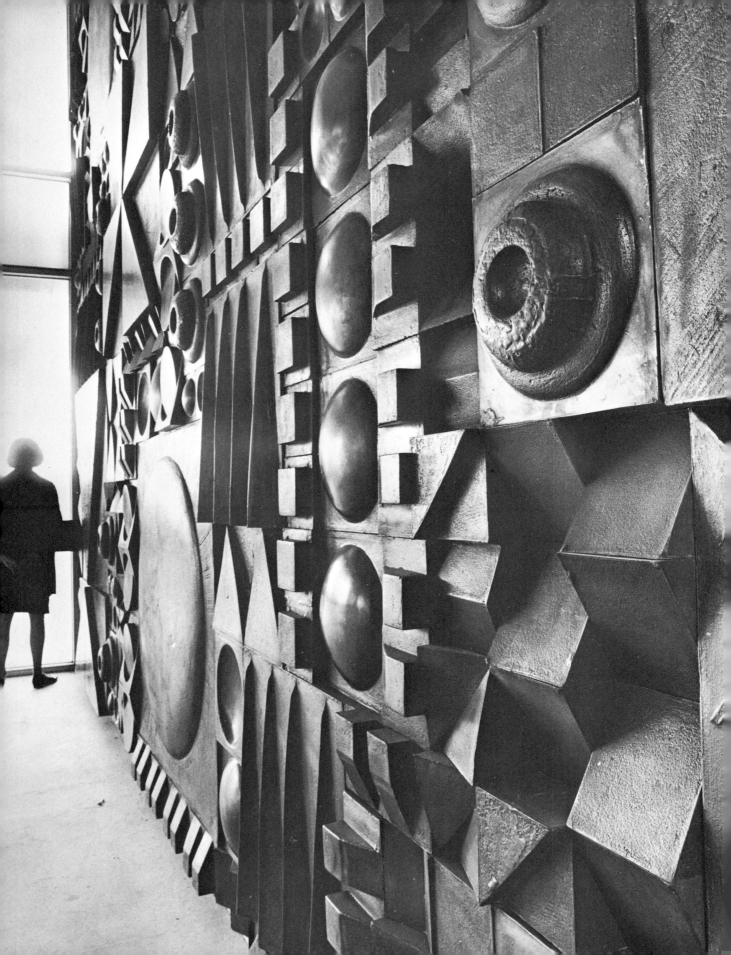

# Polyester Laminations

The use of fibreglass cloth as a reinforcement for polyester resins has long been successful in the boat building industry. This combination of materials produces a product which is strong, lightweight, and resistant to moisture and weathering. Fibreglass laminates resist the corrosive and staining effects of many chemicals, including mild acids and alkalis.

**Fibreglass Cloth**

Fibreglass cloth is the most widely used fabric for lamination and is made of glass, as its name implies. Glass is spun into fine fibers through a complex process and is then gathered and woven into fabrics of various weaves. The glass cloth is tough and flexible, and may be draped, cut with scissors, or handled in other ways like ordinary cloth. When this material is used to make lamination with polyester resin, the resin flows in and around the threads of the fibreglass cloth, which are completely imbedded in the plastic resin. Later, the hardened lamination may be sanded, filed, drilled, machined, or polished with ordinary shop tools.

**Fibreglass Mat**

Fibreglass mat is also a glass product, similar to fibreglass cloth, but is of a looser weave. When cut into small sections, it is easier to manipulate into complex molds. Both fibreglass mat and cloth are available in thicknesses ranging from lightweight to heavyweight, and in rolls 38″, 50″, 60″, and 72″ wide.

**Fibreglass Tapes**

Tapes of the above mentioned materials are available in widths ranging from ½″ to 6″ wide. The tapes may be wound around sculptural forms in building fibreglass shells, or for permanent laminations to armatures or cores.

**Other Fibreglass Materials**

Other fibreglass cloth materials include continuous strand, woven or spun rovings, chopped strand, and milled glass fibers.

Continuous strand is string-like glass fiber, supplied in continuous twisted yarn or twisted multistrand roving, wound in spools. Woven or spun rovings are heavy, coarse glass fabrics, varying in weight from 15 to 27 ounces per

**Architectural Wall** by William Mitchell, polyester and fibreglass. Various units were laminated individually, assembled like building blocks.

square yard. These fabrics are woven in many combinations of weave and impart extremely high impact strength to polyester laminations.

Chopped strands are made of continuous filament strand, cut from ¼″ to 2″ in length, and available in bulk form. Milled fibres are short, hammer-milled glass filaments ⅟₃₂″ to ⅓″ long, also available in bulk form. The milled fibers and chopped strand are useful in making pasty mixes of polyester resin for casting or for use in build-up methods over wire screen armatures.

**Lamination Methods with Polyester Resin**

There are four principle methods of polyester lamination which should be of interest to the sculptor:

(1) Laminating fibreglass cloth in molds.
(2) Permanent lamination to cores.
(3) Making fibreglass panels.
(4) Laminating dissimilar materials.

**Laminating Fibreglass Cloth with Molds**

This is a molding process in which small pieces of fibreglass cloth are cut and pressed into or over prepared molds of plaster, or other mold materials. A gel coat of catalyzed polyester resin is usually brushed into the prepared mold; this is followed by subsequent laminations of resin and glass cloth. Layers of resin and glass cloth alternate and the process is repeated until the artist obtains a shell of the desired thickness. Before beginning a lamination (or lay-up) of fibreglass, proper attention should be given to the preparation of molds for easy release of the casting. (See Chapter 20, which describes molds and releases.)

After the mold release is applied, the first coat of resin applied to the mold is called a gel coat. This initial coating of catalyzed polyester resin usually includes some thixotropic filler to give the resin more body (see fillers in Chapter 5). It is applied carefully to the mold with a brush in order to fill all surface details. Care should be taken not to disturb the mold release. After the gel coat has hardened, a second coat of catalyzed resin is brushed on, this time without the addition of thixotropic filler. Then small pieces of fibreglass cloth are cut and pressed into the wet resin with a household paint brush, the bristles of which have been cut short. Catalyzed polyester resin is then applied over the coat of fibreglass cloth. The process is repeated three or four times, until the desired thickness is obtained. Small rubber or metal rollers or squeegees are handy tools to compress laminations over large flat surfaces.

When the laminate has gelled (but not completely cured), it may be removed from the mold and trimmed. Removing the cast before it has completely cured is recommended because release is easier and trimming is easier. Of course, if you are using a plaster waste mold technique, the casting should be allowed to harden completely before the plaster mold is

**Stabile** by Robert Howard, fibreglass and polyester over balsa wood.
The lamination was executed over a lightweight balsa wood core.

**Passage Pour L'Autre Côté** by Gerard Singer, 12½' x 12' x 6', polyester
and fibreglass over metal.

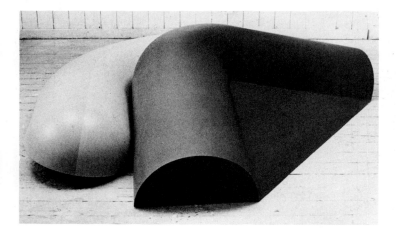

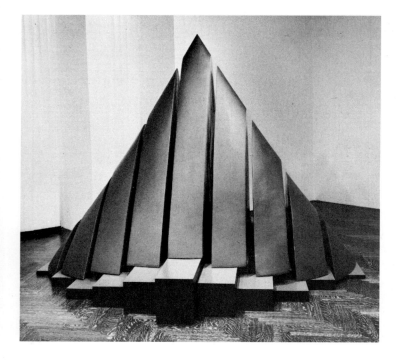

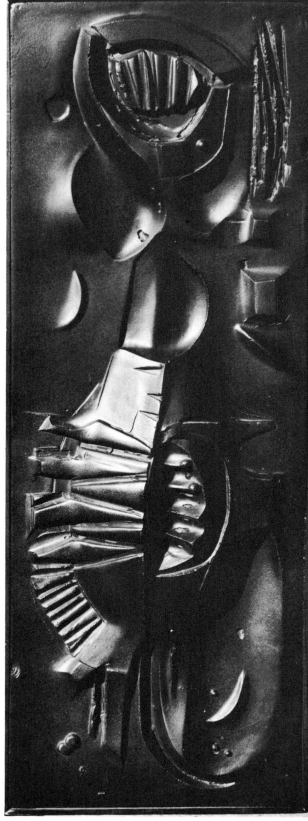

**Vantage** (upper left) by Derrick Woodham, 96″ x 60″ x 18″, painted polyester, fibreglass, and aluminum construction. The lamination is supported by lightweight aluminum.

**Through** (lower left) by Phillip King, 84″ x 108″, polyester and fibreglass, courtesy Richard Feigen Gallery, New York. The forms were laminated separately and assembled on the step-like base.

**Landscape** (right) by Nicholas Roukes, 13″ x 36″, fibreglass and polyester. From an original of pottery clay, a plaster of Paris mold was made and treated with wax and PVA release. The gel coat contained black polyester paste colorant and was followed by a series of laminations.

chipped away, to avoid any damage to the casting. Allow at least 24 hours for curing.

A plaster mold which is carefully designed to eliminate undercuts may be reused several times. Each time it is used, however, additional parting agent should be applied. Stubborn castings may be coaxed free of the rigid plaster molds by using warm water which must be poured very carefully between the cast and the mold.

Lightweight sculptural forms, or cores, are first made of wood, polyurethane, or other lightweight materials. These materials should be selected to withstand the solvent effect of styrene, which is within the polyester resin.

In this process, the core is brushed with catalyzed resin, and then fibreglass cloth, mat, or tape is pressed over it. Successive coats are built up as described a moment ago. No parting agent is necessary over the core material, as it remains permanently inside the final sculptural form. A laminating polyester resin should be used, with a final coat of surfacing resin to obtain a hard, dry surface.

**Laminating Fibreglass Cloth to Cores**

Thin, surfacing fibreglass mat is laminated with polyester resin to produce translucent panels, or plastic collages. Flat or loose materials — or even flat objects — may be sandwiched between the fibreglass matting to create many different types of effects. Rice papers, cellophanes, collage papers, photographs, drawings, threads, parts from old clocks — there is no limit — make interesting inclusions for this type of lamination.

In beginning a translucent panel, stretch a sheet of Mylar or acetate plastic over a flat work surface. Polyester resin will not stick to this material, and no parting agent is necessary. Pour some catalyzed polyester resin over the Mylar plastic, and spread it evenly with a piece of cardboard or a rubber squeegee. Then lay a sheet of fibreglass surfacing mat over the wet resin, pour an additional amount of catalyzed resin over it, and squeegee it evenly over the entire surface. Into this wet surface, the collage materials can be arranged, creating the design of the panel. Finally, place a second piece of fibreglass matting over this surface, pour more catalyzed resin over it, and lightly spread with the squeegee.

To finish the laminate, place a second piece of Mylar plastic sheeting over the laminate and apply even pressure with a rubber roller. Apply pressure from the center outward, taking care to squeeze out air bubbles while the laminate is compressed. When the resin has gelled, the top sheet of Mylar plastic may be peeled off and the edges of the laminate trimmed with a knife. Later, the second piece of plastic (beneath the laminate) is removed when the resin has hardened.

There are many variations of this method. Many layers of fibreglass matting may be built up, and ingredients such as foils, dyes, pigments, liquids,

**Laminating Translucent Panels**

and other materials can be incorporated within the panel. Heavier, three-dimensional materials should be laminated to the top surface.

**Laminating Dissimilar Materials**

Materials such as cloth, paper, wood, metal, or glass may also be laminated either to themselves or to one another. When making laminates of rigid, dissimilar materials, it is wise to use a flexible polyester resin, such as the isophthalic types. These allow for expansion and contraction of the mixed media.

Any of the polyester resins will work well in laminating flexible materials such as fabrics or papers.

**Color in Polyester Laminations**

There are two basic methods used to obtain color in fibreglass laminations:

(1) *Integral Color:* Color is mixed with the resin beforehand, using either paste, powder, or liquid color which is compatible with the polyester resin. Because the color becomes an integral part of this lamination, it cannot be removed by subsequent sanding or polishing operations. Opaque, translucent, or transparent colorants are available for polyester. (See Sources of Supplies at the end of this book.)

(2) *Surface Coatings:* Here, the laminations are painted *after* they are completed. The most permanent type of paint coating is an epoxy paint which is available from most paint or boat shops. You can also make pigmented catalyzed polyester of the same type which was used to create the lamination; this polyester coating may contain a bit more catalyst and include dry colors, pastes, or liquids which are compatible with the resin. Polyester laminations may also be painted with acrylic or vinyl paints.

**Sprayed Laminations**

A new type of spray gun has been developed which sprays catalyzed and promoted resin, while simultaneously feeding chopped fibreglass strands into the resin spray. Using this process, the sculptor may build large scale laminates very quickly. The sculptor may also *job out* the casting process by taking his prepared molds directly to a fabricator who operates such equipment. Petersen Products, 1325 Old County Road, Belmont, California, manufactures and distributes equipment of this type.

# Making a Mobile of Reinforced Polyester

4

San Francisco sculptor Robert Howard demonstrates his method of using polyester and fibreglass cloth laminations to create his mobiles. In this demonstration, he traces the development of his 12′ architectural mobile, *Comstock*, commissioned for the First National Bank of Las Vegas, Nevada.

In creating *Comstock*, my objective was to try to capture the excitement of the gold rush days with all the activity, frenzy, and seething hysteria of the old west as prospectors searched for precious gold and silver.

I visualized my sculpture with inherent physical movement — an air-motion mobile which could revolve and which would have many brilliant surfaces to capture and reflect light as it moved and fluttered in space.

I have always been fascinated by kinetic gadgets and mechanical objects of all kinds, and many years have elapsed since I constructed my first kinetic sculpture. My experimentation with motion in sculpture began in those early days when an old friend, Alexander Calder, was also deeply involved in the early phases of his work. Since then, many sculptures in many media have been conceived in this San Francisco studio.

Although I am not an engineer, I am constantly solving the ubiquitous technical problems that crop up with kinetic sculpture. Many mechanical components, connecting links, bearings, mechanical devices, and media combinations are inventions that I have had to make in order to effect balance and motion in my work.

There are several reasons why polyester is an excellent material for making mobiles. The material is light; it is quite strong; it weathers well; it can be given an attractive finish; and it is very easy to handle. Furthermore, I prefer to manage all the stages of making the sculpture myself, rather than jobbing out any particular phase of the work. Using polyester, even making architectural sculptures is possible within the studio. The plastic resin is also inexpensive when compared to the cost of traditional materials.

**Making Basic Shapes**

In beginning *Comstock*, I designed a total of 22 elements which were to comprise the total shape of the mobile. The V-shaped arms were to be of various sizes and linked together in a manner that would produce movement.

I made many preliminary sketches and finally developed a scale drawing for the basic plan of the mobile. However, to further visualize its three-dimensional form — and to also work out some of the technical problems of balance and motion — I first made a small scale model of balsa wood. The scale model measures about 24″.

I began the actual construction of *Comstock* by making full size drawings of each of the arms. These were then traced onto ⅛″ plywood, cut out with a bandsaw, and assembled to form a V-shape. To these V-shaped plywood arms, I then attached blocks of rigid polyurethane foam plastic, which were glued in place with catalyzed polyester resin. After the resin had set, I used a rasp to shape the urethane blocks, creating curvilinear sculptural planes. The rigid urethane plastic is cellular and quite easy to sand. I used this basic procedure in constructing all 22 arms of the mobile.

**Applying Fibreglass Cloth**

In the next operation, I worked on the arms of the mobile, one at a time. A liberal coat of catalyzed polyester resin was brushed over the surface, and then fibreglass cloth was pressed over it. The fibreglass cloth was trimmed as I went along. An additional coat of catalyzed polyester resin was applied to the top surface. Using a household paint brush with dabbing motions, I pressed down the glass cloth firmly, while also removing air bubbles. I worked with small batches of catalyzed polyester resin, which were mixed in paper cups. About 10 drops of MEK peroxide catalyst were used per ounce of polyester resin. The entire group of mobile arms were treated in this way and allowed to cure overnight.

It should be noted that urethane, rather than styrofoam blocks were used because this material is impervious to styrene, which is within polyester resin.

**Finishing and Assembling**

Later, each fibreglass covered element was sanded smooth with carborundum paper. For a final surface texture, I painted each arm with catalyzed polyester resin and sifted redwood sawdust over the wet surface, using a kitchen flour sifter. The resin-sawdust coating provided an attractive surface texture, which was then painted with silver vinyl paint.

In preparing for the assembly of the mobile, I drilled holes into each of the arms and installed screw eyes. Three interlocking metal rings were used as connecting links between each arm, forming a kind of chain, which allowed for adequate freedom of movement. I began assembling the mobile from the bottom up, carefully balancing each arm as the sculpture grew. In some cases, adjustments for balance had to be made. This problem was solved easily by drilling holes into the arms and inserting lead shot until the proper balance was achieved.

**Step 1:** Robert Howard completes the scale drawing for his 12′ fibreglass mobile, *Comstock*, commissioned for the First National Bank of Las Vegas, Nevada. He designed the mobile to symbolize the frantic search for gold and silver in the old west during the 1850's. In order to solve problems of balance and movement, Howard made a three-dimensional model before beginning work on the actual mobile.

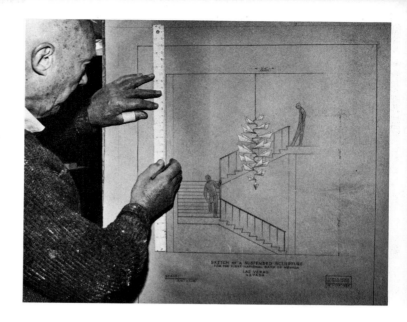

**Step 2:** The artist refines one of the arms, which has been cut and assembled from ⅛″ plywood. Rigid polyurethane blocks have been attached to the surface with catalyzed polyester resin and are shaped with a wood rasp. The mobile is composed of 22 elements (or arms) which will be linked together, allowing free movement.

**Step 3:** A liberal coating of catalyzed polyester resin is applied to the arms of the mobile, followed by fibreglass cloth, which is pressed into the wet surface. The glass cloth is trimmed as work progresses, and additional polyester resin is applied over the top surface with a brush, using a dabbing motion. Ten drops of MEK peroxide catalyst per ounce of polyester resin were used, mixed in small batches in disposable paper cups.

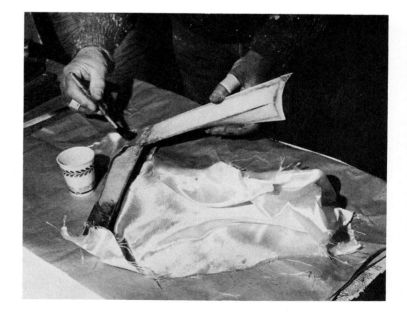

**Step 4:** After light sanding with carbide paper, the final surface texture is applied. Redwood sawdust is sifted onto wet catalyzed polyester resin, which has been liberally brushed onto each of the arms of the mobile.

**Step 5:** Howard assembles the mobile by fastening metal rings to screw eyes inserted into each arm of the sculpture. Occasionally, corrections for balance are made by drilling small holes and filling them with lead shot. The arms are then painted with silver vinyl paint.

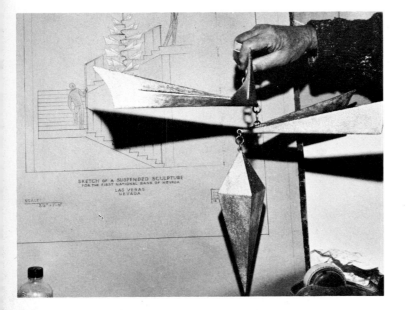

**Step 6:** The mobile is assembled from the bottom up. Here the artist compares the progress of his work with his original drawing.

**Comstock** (right) Assembly is completed on the 12′ mobile. Howard now makes minor corrections to improve balance and movement.

**Sir John Barbirolli** (detail) by Anthony Gray, 5'
high, resinated bronze. A cast of resin and bronze
powder was made from a plaster mold derived
from a clay original.

# Casting Polyester Containing Fillers  **5**

Among the many materials which may be mixed with polyester resin for casting are:

(1) Crushed granite, marble, limestone, terrazzo chips.

(2) Metallic granules, flakes, and powders such as brass, copper, bronze, nickel, aluminum, iron, lead.

(3) Bakelite microballoons (plastic spheres).

Before adding any of these materials to polyester resin for casting, the resin must first be thickened in order to suspend the heavy particles and to prevent them from settling within the mix. The sculptor may buy a commercially prepared *thixotropic paste resin,* which has already been prepared to a thick viscosity, or he may choose to make his own thixotropic polyester paste by adding fillers to polyester resins.

**Thickening the Resin**

The commercially prepared thixotropic resin is usually prepared to a consistency of petroleum jelly, or soft butter. This mixture usually contains colloidal silica (Cab-O-Sil) as a filler. Cab-O-Sil is an awkward material for the artist to handle, as it has a natural tendency to float, filling the atmosphere with minute dust particles, a serious hazard to health.

If you choose to make your own thixotropic resin, use fillers such as talc, whiting, etc., and add about 2% to 7% of the filler (by volume) to the catalyzed polyester resin. The resultant mixture should have the consistency of petroleum jelly or be even thicker if heavy particles are to be added later.

Experience has indicated that it is wise to add just enough catalyst to this thixotropic paste to provide a pot life, or working time, of about two hours. The resin-catalyst combinations should be determined empirically; a good trial combination would be about five drops of MEK peroxide catalyst to one ounce of thixotropic polyester resin. It should be noted that some of the metallic fillers inhibit the curing cycle, and larger amounts of catalyst may be required. Brass fillers, for example, will require more catalyst, while aluminum will not. For this reason, it is always a good idea to mix a small trial batch before beginning large scale operations.

**Adding Catalyst**

To insure complete dispersion of the catalyst, mix it with the thixotropic resin *first,* before adding the heavier metallic fillers or other bodies. Adding 1% or 2% of milled glass fibers will add meshing strength.

## Adding Crushed Stone

Most crushed stones or minerals may be mixed successfully with the buttery catalyzed polyester. Mesh sizes of 1 to 100 may be used. With heavier particles, more filler must be added to the resin to create a thicker paste.

## Adding Bakelite Microballoons

A syntactic plastic putty may be created by mixing plastic microballoons with catalyzed thixotropic resin. Microballoons are tiny, hollow spheres of phenolic plastic, which, when mixed with the thixotropic polyester, make a dark brown putty.

This mixture may be pressed into molds with a spatula; the same procedure is followed when one works with metallic or stone mixtures.

The proportions of crushed stone or microballoons added to catalyzed thixotropic resin may be varied in order to produce required effects and densities. Mixtures may be made simply by using a stick or a spatula. Special electric mixers, with kneading action mixing blades, are available for large scale operations.

## Adding Metallic Granules

The technique of mixing metallic granules, powders, and flakes with polyester has been in use for some time in England. Sculpture of this type is usually referred to as *cold metal casting* or *resinated metal casting*. To conserve the amount of metallic filler used, only a gel coat of resinated metal need be applied to molds. Subsequent coats of regular thixotropic resin — without metallic additives — are applied over this to build up the required thickness and strength.

Proportions of polyester resin and metallic fillers may need to be varied in order to meet the requirements of the specific task. A good basic formula to use is three parts of metal (by weight) to one part of the catalyzed thixotropic polyester resin. After mixing a small trial batch, adjustments may then be made to control the final quality and cure cycle. The sculptor's needs may vary from a mixture which has some flow — in order to be cast into intricate molds — to a pastier mix to be used for molding and which will hold to a vertical wall without shifting.

Metallic granules of at least 100 mesh are recommended, obtainable from the Metals Disintegrating Company of Elizabeth, New Jersey. The metallic powders commonly used for making paints are too fine for this use.

It should also be mentioned that some metallic fillers are lighter than others and the required proportions of resin and metallic fillers will also vary. Aluminum powder, for example, is quite light; 1½ parts of aluminum filler to one part of resin may be quite sufficient. On the other hand, bronze powder is quite heavy. In this case, about 5 parts of metallic filler to one part of resin may be about right. Room temperature for using resinated metal should be about 70°F. The technique of using resinated metal for casting is described in Chapter 6, in which Jonathan Batchelor shows how he casts a figure using this method.

In combining stone, microballoons or metallic granules with resins, the following procedure is recommended. First, thicken the resin (if not already thickened). Add the catalyst to the thixotropic polyester resin and mix thoroughly. Then add the stone, microballoons, or metallic granules to obtain the required viscosity and textural effects.

**Summary of Procedure**

Chemicals normally employed for coloring traditional metal sculpture may also be used for resinated metal casts. Stronger chemical concentrations are usually required, and surfaces should be etched first or rubbed with steel wool or wet sanded to expose the metallic particles to the action of the chemicals. Strong concentrations of hydrochloric acid produce an excellent green patina on resinated bronze castings; however, chemicals of this sort are hazardous and are not recommended for general studio use because they tend to pit the resin surface. Organic acids have been found to create interesting color without damaging or pitting the resin surface. In general, successful patination of resinated metal by chemical means is a delicate job, as the resin tends to protect metal particles, and heavy concentrations of mineral acids attack resin surfaces.

**Surface Patinas for Resinated Metal**

Non-acid finishes for resinated metal sculpture include black stove polish, chrome polishes, and waxes which contain oil color or dry pigment. A polyester patina may be created by using catalyzed polyester resin, mixed with dry color and applied to the surface of the sculpture. A cloth, saturated with lacquer thinner or acetone, can then be used to remove some the patina from the salient points of the sculpture before the patina has gelled. This process may be repeated several times with a variety of colors in order to build a final effect.

The materials listed in this chapter may be pressed into a variety of molds, which are listed and described in Chapter 20. Plaster molds, which are most commonly used, should be allowed to dry thoroughly and then lacquered three or four times. Follow this with a heavy coat of wax mold release, and then polish. Finally, apply two coats of polyvinyl alcohol (PVA mold release) with either a brush or a spray gun.

**Preparing Plaster Molds for Casting**

Approximately 24 hours should be allowed for curing before the casting is removed. In waste molds of plaster, the mold is chiseled away to release the casting. Flexible mold materials present no problems because the casting literally drops out of the mold.

**Removing and Refining Castings**

Filled polyester castings are strong and durable and may be refined with metal files, carbide paper, or other shop tools. A protective face mask should be worn to protect the sculptor from plastic dust if he is doing excessive sanding. This dust is irritating to the lungs. Wet sanding is suggested to alleviate this condition.

**Two Women at a Table** (upper left) by Arlene Love, life size, polyester, courtesy Terry Dintenfass Gallery, New York. Another example of sculpture which combines polyester and fibreglass with coloring material that becomes integral with the liquid resin.

**Two Figures** (lower left) by Anthony Weller, 4′ high, resinated aluminum. Originally modeled in clay, the sculpture was cast from a prepared plaster of Paris mold, using a fibreglass lay-up with a gel coat of resin mixed with powdered aluminum.

**Mervyn Levy** (above right) by Anthony Gray, life size, resinated bronze. A plaster mold was made from the clay original and a cast was made from resin mixed with bronze powder. The texture of the clay is faithfully preserved.

**Couple** (right) by Anthony Weller, 12″ high, resinated bronze. Cast in resin and bronze powder, this figure has the metallic luminosity of bronze.

# 6 Casting a Figure with Polyester-metal

Jonathan Batchelor of Canyon, California, describes a method of casting resinated metal, a technique combining polyester resin with fine granules of metal. The catalyzed polyester-metal paste is pressed into a plaster mold and allowed to cure at room temperature. His demonstration sculpture, *Requiem*, was cast with bronze metallic granules of 101 mesh, mixed with a catalyzed thixotropic polyester.

In creating *Requiem*, I merged a traditional method with a contemporary medium, polyester resin, and discovered that working with this material is indeed exciting. Many possibilities for expression are inherent in its use.

I do not feel that resinated metal casting is an imitative technique. Rather than an attempt to duplicate bronze casting, this is bronze casting in yet another form. In this cold metal casting technique, no heat or crucibles are required. Bronze is disintegrated into minute granules, rather than melted, and then is mixed with thixotropic polyester resin. This mixture is then pressed into molds at ordinary room temperature and produces castings which are as strong as metal. (Metallic granules for casting with polyester are available from Metals Disintegrating Company of Elizabeth, New Jersey; particles from fine to coarse mesh, in a variety of metals.)

Among the advantages of resinated metal are:

(1) *Strength:* Castings exhibit excellent impact and tensile strength and also display good weathering characteristics.

(2) *Lightweight:* Working with a lightweight material means that transportation and handling bills are lighter too. Sculpture commissions which would not be feasible if one used traditional methods may be possible with this medium.

(3) *Beauty:* There are many types of metallic granules available for this method. The granules may be mixed independently, or mixed together to produce intermediate metallic hues. Patinas (chemical or other types) are easily applied to resinated metal sculpture for polychromatic surfaces.

(4) *Ease of handling:* There is no need to call upon a foundry. All of the processes necessary to complete the sculpture and casting may be accomplished within the sculptor's studio.

In describing the means by which I completed *Requiem*, I shall arbitrarily divide the work into five principal stages: (1) constructing the armature;

(2) modeling the clay figure; (3) making a plaster waste mold; (4) preparing the resinated metal; (5) applying the final surface patina.

**Constructing the Armature**

Commercially prepared armatures for modeling figures are available at most art supply stores; however, I prefer to make my own, following a method which I have used successfully for many years. It is probably the simplest, least expensive armature designed. For this figure, I used ¾" plywood to make a base measuring 15" x 20". A piece of pine, 2" x 4" x 16", was screwed to this base and a smaller piece of wood was nailed to the 2" x 4" to provide additional height and support. The entire armature was shellacked twice.

**Modeling the Clay Figure**

Much has been written regarding philosophies of creating sculpture. It is sufficient to say that the sculptor should not content himself solely with the task of attempting to reproduce the human figure in clay, but he should express his personality, his poetry, or his experience through the three-dimensional medium. I believe Maillol said, "It is nothing to copy the nude; the essential task before the artist it to express a concept or idea; to make tangible the intangibles. . . ."

In *Requiem,* I sought to express an idea through the symbol of a human figure. I chose not to use a life model, relying instead on impulse and intuition, recalling my knowledge of anatomy gained through many years of painting and sculpting. The idea was vague in the beginning, but became clearer as the work progressed. A great variety of changes was made, many of them drastic ones.

Water base sculpture clay was used to model the figure. In the beginning stages, care was taken to pack the clay tightly against the wooden armature. As the masses of form gradually developed, primary consideration was given to establishing the general volumes, the basic gesture and composition. My fingers were the only tools used in this preliminary stage of the work. Later, a large wire loop was also employed.

As the work progressed, I deliberately sought simplicity of form and line. I placed the sculpture on a turntable and worked at it from many sides, clarifying and developing planes and angles, solid and open forms, concave and convex shape relationships. Above all, I sought to develop a simple, lyrical transition of the various elements of the sculpture. Later, the clay surface was treated with a notched wire loop tool to prevent an overly smooth quality.

**Making Plaster Waste Molds**

As the name implies, this is a "one-shot" process. Only one casting is made, replacing the modeled clay sculpture with a casting of resinated metal. For making *more* than one copy of an original sculpture, piece molds, or flexible molds should be used.

As *Requiem* was fairly complex, a total of five sections was made for the waste mold. I began making the mold by isolating one section of the sculpture with thin clay slabs. Casting plaster was mixed in a small rubber bowl and applied to the walled off section with a spatula. Plaster was applied in successive coats to build a mold thickness of about ½". Next, the clay retaining walls were removed and the edges of the plaster were notched in several places with the end of a kitchen knife, producing small hollows. The adjacent mold section was made with small projections to fit the hollows and insure perfect registration of the two sections. Another section was walled off and the process repeated. To keep the sections of the plaster mold from sticking to each other where they butted together, clay slip was painted along the edges of each section.

After all five sections of the plaster mold were completed, they were removed from the sculpture, thoroughly washed with soap and water, and allowed to dry.

## Preparing the Mold for Casting

In order to keep resinated metal from sticking to molds, it is necessary to use a mold release over the plaster surface. I prepared my molds in the following manner. After all the mold sections were bone dry, they were given three coats of clear lacquer. This sealed the porosity of the plaster. Next, a mold release paste was applied, allowed to dry, and then polished with a soft cloth; this operation was repeated twice. Finally, two coats of polyvinyl alcohol (PVA) were brushed over the polished surfaces. The edges of the mold sections were also sealed and treated with this mold release.

## Preparing the Resinated Metal Mixture

The casting mix contains the following ingredients: (1) thixotropic polyester; (2) MEK peroxide catalyst; (3) bronze metallic granules, 101 mesh.

I used commercially prepared thixotropic polyester resin, which has a thick consistency like that of soft butter. This thickened polyester amalgam is necessary to keep heavy metallic particles in suspension; they would sink in unthickened polyester. I also wished to create a putty-like consistency which I could trowel onto the mold. I used the following mixing order in preparing the resinated metal:

(1) To 10 ounces of thixotropic polyester resin, I added 50 drops of MEK peroxide catalyst (5 drops per ounce of resin). This was thoroughly mixed into the thixotropic resin.

(2) 50% (by weight) of bronze metallic granules were added to the mixture and stirred to create an even, buttery mixture.

(3) This mixture was then applied to the plaster mold with a spatula. It should be noted that many small successive batches were mixed — rather than a few large ones — to insure adequate mixing with the catalyst, and for easier handling. Room temperature was about 70°F.

In a normal room temperature of 70°F., this mixture provided a pot life of about 30 minutes. Casting 10 ounces of resinated metal at a time gave me enough plastic to cover each individual mold section separately.

Preliminary plastic mixtures (with metallic filler) were applied directly with a spatula and built to ⅜″ thicknesses. Then came a second application of thixotropic polyester resin *without* metallic filler, and a final thickness of about ¼″ was created. These plastic mixes were applied *carefully* to each mold section to avoid getting the resinated metal over the edges. After all of the sections were cast, they were joined together with an application of resinated metal, which was applied (like an adhesive) to the seams, working from the inside of the mold, using a long handled brush.

Ten hours were allowed for curing. Then the plaster waste mold was chipped away to reveal the sculpture. I used a dull chisel and a wooden mallet to break the plaster carefully away. The cast sculpture was washed thoroughly in warm water to remove traces of the polyvinyl alcohol film. Seam marks were sanded down with carborundum paper, and the entire sculpture was rubbed briskly with steel wool to bring out the metallic quality of the casting.

**Casting the Resinated Metal**

To achieve the final patina for *Requiem,* dry colors were mixed with unthickened catalyzed polyester resin. Several thin layers of green, brown, and blue polyester patinas were applied. Between applications, some of the patina was removed with a cloth saturated in acetone.

**Final Surface Patina**

**Step 1:** Jonathan Batchelor built a simple, inexpensive armature, using two pieces of 2″ x 4″ pine, which were securely attached to a wooden base. He then gives the armature two coats of shellac to seal it against the moisture of the clay.

**Step 2:** The sculptor uses water base clay and packs it tightly against the armature. In the early stages of the work, he uses only his hands to establish the general volumes.

**Step 3:** As Batchelor adds additional clay, the sculpture begins to assume a triangular composition. Work progresses rapidly as he establishes the basic gesture of the figure.

**Step 4:** As the desired forms are achieved, he smoothes the surface with his fingers. Placed on a turntable, the emerging figure is worked on from every side as the artist seeks to clarify the developing planes and angles.

**Step 5:** Here is the completed sculpture, *Requiem*, as it appeared in final clay form. A toothed wire loop tool has been used to create surface texture. *Requiem* is a sensitively conceived work, a lyrical interplay of sculptural volumes and rhythmic lines.

**Step 6:** In making the waste mold, Batchelor isolates one section of the sculpture by pressing thin strips of clay against the figure. Five such sections were isolated and cast to make the completed mold.

**Step 7:** Plaster of Paris is mixed in a rubber bowl and then applied with a wooden spatula to the sectioned-off area of the clay figure. Care is taken to insure that the plaster covers the surface properly. Successive coats are applied to this section, building a mold thickness of about ½″, before proceeding to the next section.

**Step 8:** Here is the completed waste mold. Approximately one hour is allowed for the plaster to set and then each section of the mold is carefully removed from the clay sculpture. The mold sections are washed thoroughly and allowed to dry for several days.

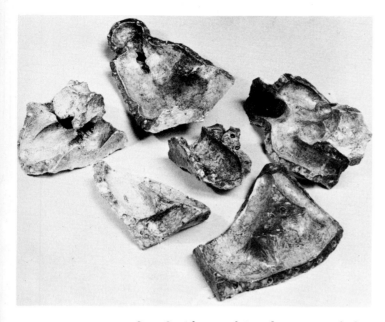 

**Step 9:** After applying three coats of clear lacquer to the dry mold sections, Batchelor then applies two coats of mold release paste, allowing each coat to dry, and polishing after each application. Finally, two coats of polyvinyl alcohol are brushed over the polished surfaces. (Although one of the mold sections broke during handling, it was easily repaired with Elmer's Glue.)

**Step 10:** Bronze metallic powder is mixed with catalyzed thixotropic polyester resin and is applied with a spatula to the mold. The thick resinated metal is easily applied and is given a pot life of approximately 30 minutes. All five sections are cast separately, assembled, and then joined with resinated metal, applied (like glue) to the seams from inside the mold. After 24 hours of curing, the waste mold is chipped away to reveal the plastic casting.

**Requiem** (right) by Jonathan Batchelor, cast of metallic filled polyester, is approximately 18″ high with a patina of blue-greens, created by mixing dry colors with catalyzed polyester resin. (See plate in color section.)

# 7 Casting a Head with Polyester Resin

In this chapter, the author demonstrates a method of casting thixotropic polyester resin into a plaster waste mold.

The term, *thixotropic*, refers to a thickened polyester resin. In this instance, polyester resin has been thickened to a paste consistency for easier application to vertical surfaces within the interior of the plaster mold. Fillers such as Cab-O-Sil, a colloidal silica, are generally mixed with polyester resin to create this thicker consistency. The resin usually has a petroleum jelly-like appearance and viscosity; the thick masses of catalyzed resin are applied with a spatula or a brush. The thick resin clings to the vertical walls of the mold without slipping and does not settle or change shape.

Because of the heavy consistency, crushed stone or other heavy bodied material may also be added to the mix if desired, without danger of the materials migrating or settling within the mixture. Sculptors have successfully cast crushed limestone, granite, marble, and similar materials with mesh sizes varying from 80 mesh to #1 size terrazzo chip.

In casting the head *Kathleen* I used a commercially prepared thixotropic polyester resin. The casting produced a very desirable surface quality, which had a translucent, ivory-like character.

The work in this demonstration chapter is divided into four principal stages: (1) constructing the armature; (2) modeling the clay head; (3) making and preparing the plaster mold; (4) casting and polishing.

**Constructing the Armature**

Before making the armature or beginning the clay sculpture, I made numerous drawings from the model. This familiarized me with the general features of the model's head and also helped me to determine the general composition of the sculpture. In this stage, decisions were made as to the gesture of the head and how much of the head and neck would be modeled. These decisions determined the proportions and size of the armature which was to be constructed.

I have found that it is wise to spend a little extra time constructing a solid armature at the outset, to avoid engineering difficulties later. Once the work is in progress, it is difficult to rectify these mechanical problems.

In preparing the armature or interior support for the clay sculpture, I used a threaded ¾ ″ pipe which was attached to a flange and then screwed securely to a wooden base made of ¾ ″ plywood. The threaded pipe was cut to 18″ in length and served as the principal supporting post for the clay sculpture. For additional support, I inserted heavy aluminum wire loops into the top of the pipe. Finally, wooden *butterflies* were tied to the aluminum wire loops as shown in the photograph. Butterflies are small X-shaped pieces of wood, tied to the wire loops with copper wire. Finally, the entire armature was given a coat of shellac and allowed to dry.

**Modeling the Head**

Prepared water base sculpture clay was packed onto the armature post and around the butterflies. No detail was attempted. My purpose was only to build up a general form which, when completed, was allowed to set, or harden slightly, before the actual modeling began.

Initially, the modeling was meant to establish correct volume relationships of the large, essential forms. The shape and angle of the head, neck, and hair were modeled and the essential planes were determined. Clay was added continually, subtracted, and added again in these early stages. Large volumes, then successively smaller ones, were defined as the work continued. Thumbs and fingers were the chief sculpture tools. Later, wire loop tools were also used. The sculptor should remember that as he works with three-dimensional material, he is continually manipulating volume, displacing space, and arranging light, as he establishes the forms, planes, and textures of his work.

If work with the water based clay is halted temporarily, it is imperative that the sculpture be covered with a damp cloth to prevent the clay from drying out. For additional insurance, it is also advisable to drape a sheet of flexible plastic over the sculpture. Keeping the clay moist is important because water based (pottery) clay has a tendency to shrink and lose its workable quality as it becomes harder.

In locating the eyes, clay was scooped away from the sculpture with the thumbs, establishing hollow recesses into which the eyes were eventually modeled. The pupils and irises of the eyes were created by using a small wire loop tool to cut away small concave shapes.

As the features were established, their relationship to the head and to each other was carefully noted. Since the demonstration sculpture, *Kathleen*, is life size, a pair of wooden calipers was used to check proportions as the work progressed.

I turned the sculpture continually on a metal turntable to check and work on it from many sides. As the work continued, an effort was made to emphasize the long, flowing lines of the hair, and to simplify sculptural forms. The final surface texture of the face was created with a notched wire loop tool; hair texture was created with a pointed orange stick.

**Making the Plaster Waste Mold**

The waste mold process is, as its name implies, a "one-shot" process in which only one casting is to be made. The first step in making the mold is to insert metal *shims* into the surface of the clay sculpture, dividing it into two halves. I used thin aluminum sheet metal, cut from TV dinner trays. Small rectangular shapes, about 1½" by 2", were cut, inserted into the clay sculpture, and overlapped to form a continuous line as shown in the photograph. A few of the metal shims were bent to a V-shape before they were inserted, serving to interlock and *register* the two sections of the mold after it was made. The shims were lightly oiled and the sculpture was then placed in a large cardboard box on the turntable, ready for making the plaster mold.

Casting plaster was sifted into a container that was a little less than half full of water. The plaster was sifted into the water slowly until it began to build up from the bottom, forming peaks through the top surface of the water. It was allowed to slake (soak) for a minute or two, and then was mixed until an even, homogeneous consistency was achieved.

The plaster should have a viscosity approaching that of heavy cream. Once the water has been added to the plaster, an irrevocable chemical action has been set into motion, and a limited time is available for the sculptor to do his work. Although there is no need to panic, the artist must work quickly and efficiently.

The plaster was flicked onto the surface of the clay sculpture, by cupping the hand (held in a downward position) and quickly opening it. In this manner, the plaster was flicked onto the entire surface of the sculpture to a thickness of approximately ¼". First one side was covered, then the turntable was revolved and the other side was covered. The sculptor will eventually learn to control the sharp, flicking wrist action so that difficult areas will be easily covered with plaster.

The first coat was allowed to set; this took about 15 minutes. Then a second mixture of plaster was made, containing more plaster than water, thus forming a thicker paste. This pastier mix was troweled—with the palm of the hand — onto the previously applied plaster, building up the thickness of the plaster mold to about ¾". The plaster should be applied in an even manner, so that a uniform thickness is created. The metal shims should not be covered.

As the plaster hardens, it goes through a chemical action that produces heat. When the plaster cools, it has set and the metal shims may be removed. To separate the two halves of the plaster mold from the clay sculpture, the metal shims were removed with pliers and water was poured into the seam to loosen the plaster mold; then small wooden wedges were used to gently pry open the two halves of the mold. To free the front section of the mold, it was necessary to use a large wire loop tool to dig away the clay. The two halves of the mold were washed with soap and water and allowed to dry.

The dry mold was prepared for casting in the manner described by Jonathan Batchelor in Chapter 6. First, the plaster was sealed by brushing three coats of clear lacquer over the surface, allowing each coat to dry between applications. These were followed by two coats of paste wax, which were polished after each application. The final step in preparing the mold was to apply two coats of PVA mold release (polyvinyl alcohol) with a brush, although smoother applications can be made by spraying. The mold was now ready for casting.

As I mentioned earlier, the sculptor may choose to make his own polyester paste by using fillers (described in Chapter 5) which are mixed with catalyzed polyester resin. The commercially prepared thixotropic polyester resins save a lot of trouble, and seem to work extremely well. Also, it is easy enough to add more polyester resin or additional fillers to this mixture to further control viscosity. Thixotropic polyester resins are available in most plastic or boat shops.

In casting the head of *Kathleen,* I used commercially prepared paste, mixing only 15 ounces at a time. To each ounce of thixo-resin, I added 10 drops of MEK peroxide catalyst, stirring it well into the resin. It is advisable to experiment beforehand with catalyst-resin combinations, taking into consideration the type of filler used, temperature, and weather conditions, as these have a marked effect on the cure cycle. My mixture produced a pot life of two hours, which gave me plenty of time to work without haste. A faster cure may produce undesirable side effects, such as warping or cracking.

The catalyzed thixotropic resin was applied to the two halves of the prepared mold with a large bristle brush; surface detail was filled carefully. Successive batches of resin were mixed and applied, eventually developing a thickness of about ½". Both sections of the mold were cast in this manner, and I was especially careful to see that resin was not allowed to spill over the edges into the seam.

When the resin had gelled, the two sections of the mold were tied together and the mold was turned on its side so I could reach in through the opening beneath. Additional catalyzed resin was brushed into the seams from the inside, joining the two cast sections together. Lacquer thinner was used to clean up the brush, and the casting was allowed to cure overnight.

Using a dull chisel and a wooden mallet, I chipped the plaster mold away carefully. The slight shrinkage of the casting made it easier to remove the plaster mold.

The casting was cleaned with soap and water and then polished with a coat of liquid plastic polish, which was rubbed briskly with a soft cloth. Liquid polishes for plastic surfaces normally contain paraffin or carnauba wax and are available at boat or paint shops. I used Formula Five Clean and Glaze Wax (made by Costa Chemicals, Laguna Beach, California), which also contains a mild amount of abrasive.

The cast sculpture possesses a milky translucence, which is inherent in this particular thixotropic polyester. Light partially enters the surface, producing a very handsome surface quality.

**Casting with Polyester Resin**

**Removing the Plaster Mold**

**Step 1:** The armature for the life size head of *Kathleen* is made of ¾" threaded pipe, attached to a flange and a plywood base. Wooden *butterflies* are attached to aluminum wire loops, inserted into the top of the pipe, and used to hold the clay.

**Step 2:** A variety of wire loop tools is used to model the head. The sculpture is placed on a turntable to facilitate work during the various stages of development. Water base clay is used to model the head.

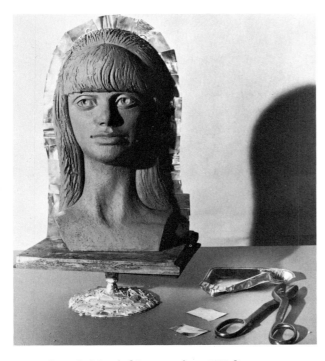

**Step 3:** Metal *shims,* cut from TV dinner trays, are inserted into the soft clay, dividing the sculpture into two halves. An occasional shim is bent into a V-shape to insure registration of the plaster mold.

**Step 4:** Before construction is begun on the mold, the sculpture is placed in a large cardboard box. Plaster of Paris is mixed to a creamy consistency and applied by cupping the hand and sharply flicking the plaster onto the surface of the sculpture.

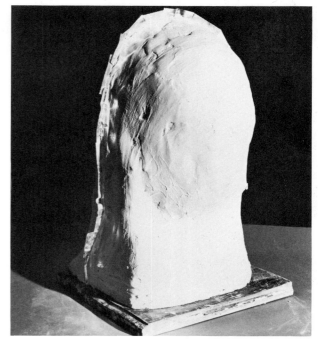

**Step 5:** Both sides of the head are covered with an initial coating of plaster, about ¼″ thick. The plaster is then allowed to set before a second coat is applied.

**Step 6:** The second batch of plaster is mixed to a very thick consistency and applied over the first coat, with the hand acting as a trowel. The final mold thickness is approximately ¾″.

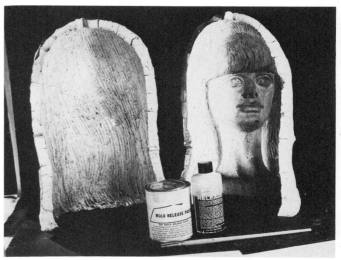

**Step 7:** Pliers are used to remove the metal shims from the mold and small wooden wedges are forced into the open seam to help pry apart the two sections. Soap and warm water are used to wash the mold and then it is allowed to dry thoroughly.

**Step 8:** The mold release consists of three coats of clear lacquer applied to the inside of the mold, followed by two applications of mold release wax and two coats of polyvinyl alcohol.

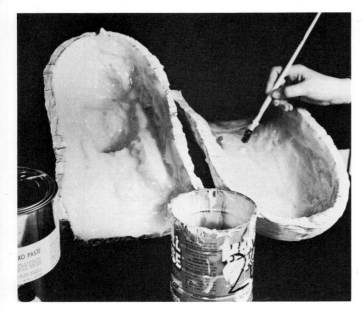

**Step 9:** Catalyzed thixotropic polyester resin is applied to the two sections of the mold with a long handled bristle brush. Many small batches of resin are mixed and applied, building a thickness of about ½".

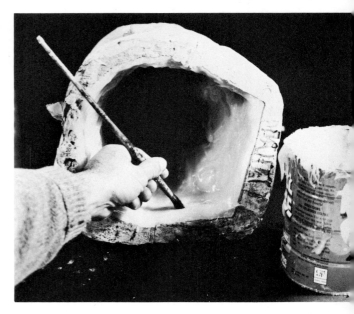

**Step 10:** The two parts of the mold are tied together; additional catalyzed thixotropic polyester resin is applied to the seams from within, joining the two cast sections.

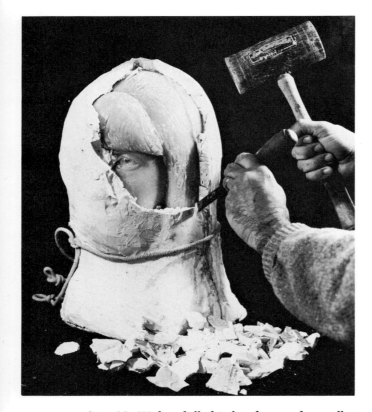

**Step 11:** With a dull chisel and a wooden mallet, the plaster mold is carefully chipped away to reveal the polyester sculpture. The work is then washed with warm water and soap and polished with wax.

**Kathleen** (right) by Nicholas Roukes, **life size**, polyester. (See plate in color section.)

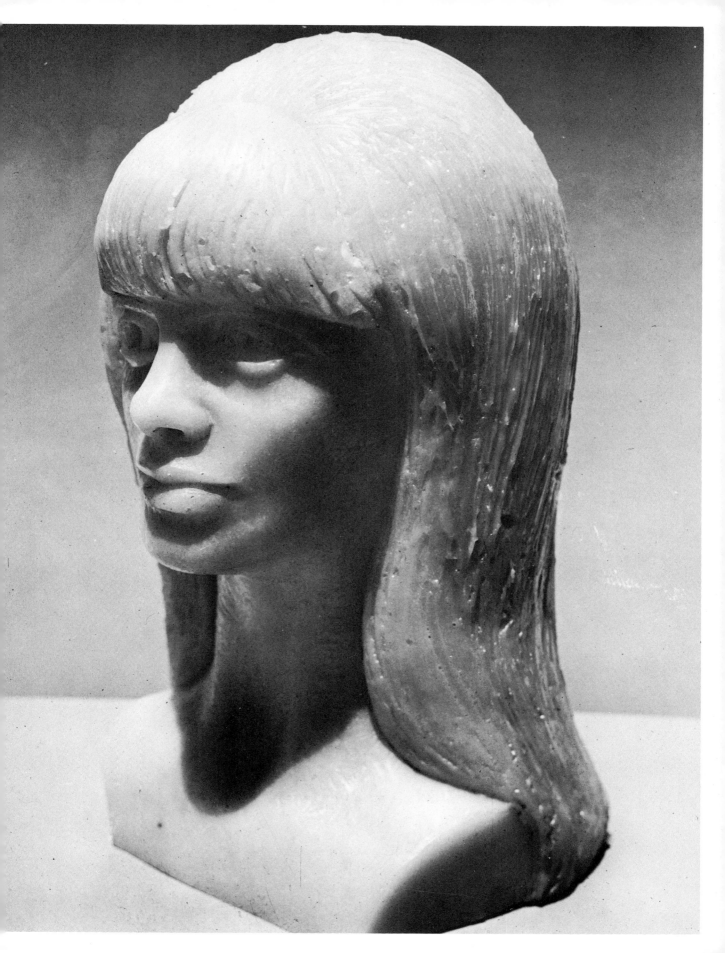

# 8 Modeling with Polyester Putty

St. Maur, one of France's leading artists doing research in synthetic materials for sculpture, demonstrates a method of using polyester putty of clay-like consistency to create an abstract sculpture.

Commercially available plastic putties, suitable for techniques similar to the one described in this chapter, are discussed in Chapter 9.

Before explaining my method of working with polyester putty, I should mention that the inspiration for my sculpture came from Arthur Rimbaud's poem, "A Season in Hell," an eloquent, penetrating interpretation concerning the meaning of life. Rimbaud continually asks: Who is man? Where is he? Is he buffoon, prophet, or angel?

To summarize briefly the concept of my sculpture, *The Tomb* signifies man's transit from one human condition to another, from one epoch to another. Man resides temporarily in a tomb, between heaven and hell. His movements are guided by the rudder of human sensibility and by energy forces that are generated from within his being. He charts his course and attempts to guide his tomb towards the sun. Each moment he moves he destroys past moments, ever becoming, ever passing through conditions of heaven and hell. The moving tomb is a metaphor of man imprisoned, and yet free, of his delicate, fleeting life, and of his yearning to transcend himself and his environment.

I have attempted to symbolize this idea in my sculpture by dividing the work into five separate, yet combined forms: the sky, the tomb, the earth, the rudder, and the sensibilities. Each has a specific form and a specific color.

I began the work by sketching, by making many visual interpretations of the idea. I was satisfied with one of the sketches, and proceeded to develop the concept in its three-dimensional state.

**Making an Armature of Wire Screen**

Taking a pair of wire cutters and some wire screen, I cut many shapes, following the suggestions of my drawings. Since I was using light wire, the shapes were easily formed by hand and joined together. A tube of manila paper was inserted into one of the wire screen shapes for temporary support.

After the sections of wire screen were tied together securely and the armature was completely assembled, I turned to the task of preparing the polyester putties. I wanted this sculpture to have brilliant integral colors of red, yellow, and blue, in addition to black and white. During the years that I have been working with polyester, I have experimented and developed many variations of pastes and putties. One of my thixotropic putties, Polybeton, is sold commercially in France, and constitutes the base for the polychromatic putties which I used in this demonstration.

To a polyester resin, thickened to buttery consistency with organic or inorganic fillers, dry color is added and mixed thoroughly, producing a heavy, colored batter. An entire palette of the required colored pastes is prepared on a large piece of plywood. A separate board — the "dough board" — is covered with talc for the final preparation of the putties.

A small amount of colored putty is picked up with a spatula and patted into a pancake shape on the talc surface. Some catalyst (in a jelly state) is troweled over the surface of the putty and the pancake is then folded over itself, sprinkled with talc, and kneaded many times. Protective throw-away gloves should be worn while preparing and using the colored putties.

**Preparation of Polychromatic Polyester Putties**

Black catalyzed putty was rolled out into a long, snake-like coil, and pressed onto the wire screen, outlining essential shapes, like the leading of stained glass. The putty hardened in 20 minutes. Using the same method to prepare the other colored putties, I applied them to the screen from the bottom upwards, using a small palette knife. One after another, the colors were mixed and applied to the wire screen, until the entire surface area was covered. A long stick was used to apply the catalyzed putty to the interior of the large, central shape after the exterior had hardened and the temporary manila paper support could be removed.

As a final polish, the sculpture was given two coats of mildly abrasive carnauba paste wax, and a brisk rubbing.

**Applying the Putties**

St. Maur discusses some of the preliminary sketches for his polyester sculpture, *The Tomb,* inspired by Arthur Rimbaud's poem, "A Season in Hell."

Step 1: The sculptor cuts and shapes wire mesh, developing the idea into three-dimensional form.

Step 2: The essential forms of the sculpture are tied together with wire and a tube of manila paper is inserted into the largest shape to give temporary support.

**Step 3:** St. Maur mixes polyester resin with filler and pigment to obtain a pasty batter. Brilliant pastes of red, yellow, blue, white, and black are prepared in this manner.

**Step 4:** A small quantity of the prepared paste is patted out on the "dough board," a talc-covered wooden surface. Catalyst is added to the polyester paste, and the sculptor kneads the mixture over the talc to a doughy consistency.

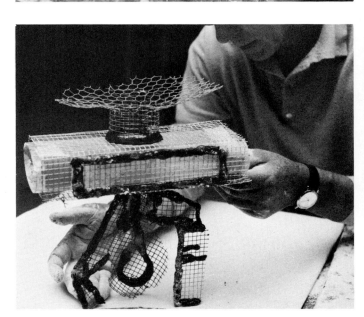

**Step 5:** The artist applies a black catalyzed polyester putty to the wire screen surface and contemplates the application of the next color paste. The mixtures are catalyzed and prepared in small quantities as the work progresses, and are applied to the armature with a small spatula.

# Commercially Available Plastic Pastes and Putties

# 9

Many synthetic pastes, marketed for making general household repairs, are available in hardware and paint stores. They are available as plastic wood, plastic metal, liquid solder, liquid steel, etc. They may be purchased in tubes or in larger quantities directly from the manufacturers. No catalyst is necessary for many of these materials, as most of them are made of a nitrocellulose base and harden by exposure to air.

**Synthetic Automotive Body Putties**

Synthetic automotive body putties are generally made of an epoxy resin base, and require the addition of a hardener; the resin then *polymerizes* to a rock hard surface. These epoxy resins are excellent for use in sculpture, and may be applied to practically any non-greasy surface: metal, wood, styrofoam, polyurethane, papier maché, concrete, etc. They can be applied over armatures and later painted, or pigments and fillers may be incorporated directly into the resin for integral color. After hardening, the body putties may be drilled, sanded, filed, tapped, buffed, and polished with ordinary wood or metal working tools.

Epoxy automotive body putties are available in most paint stores and automotive supply houses.

**Heavy Bodied Thixotropic Polyester Pastes**

The nature of these materials has been described in detail in Chapter 7, "Casting a Head with Polyester Resin." Heavy bodied thixotropic polyester pastes are available from boat repair shops.

**Acrylic Paste Extender**

This extender is made of acrylic emulsion, is thickened with a filler such as marble dust, and is used widely by artists to create textures on paintings. This material lends itself to the build-up method in sculpture as well, but should be applied in thinner layers to avoid surface cracking.

Acrylic paste extender is available in most art stores as an accessory item for acrylic paints. The acrylic paint, incidentally, may be mixed with the extender to make polychromatic pastes.

---

**The Tomb** by St. Maur, polyester, approximately 14″ high. *The Tomb,* begins to assume its final shape and color as the artist continues to apply additional catalyzed polyester putty to the surface. (See plate in color section.)

**Sculpmetal**

This is a plastic aluminum paste manufactured by the Sculpmetal Company of Pittsburgh, Pennsylvania. This material may be applied directly over wire armatures with brush or spatula, and hardens without the use of a catalyst. It may also be thinned with Sculpmetal solvent and applied by brush over sculpture made of plaster, bisque fired clay, concrete, or wood. It dries hard in 1-24 hours, depending upon the thickness of the application.

The Woodhill Chemical Company of Cleveland, Ohio, manufactures several plastic pastes which offer excellent possibilities for sculpture. Among these are Duro Plastic Aluminum, Liquid Steel, and a plastic paste unceremoniously dubbed Gook. These materials may be applied to any non-oily surface and air dry without the addition of a hardening agent.

**Epoxy Resin Base Putties**

The Devcon Corporation of Danvers, Massachusetts, manufactures epoxy resin base putties containing approximately 20% epoxy and 80% metallic bodies. Kits are available which include the epoxy metal putty, hardening agent, mold release, and instructions.

Their products include: Plastic Steel A, Plastic Steel B (liquid), Devcon F Aluminum Putty, Devcon F-2 and F-3 Aluminum Putty (liquid), Devcon ST Steel Putty, Devcon BR Bronze Putty, Devcon L Lead Putty, and several other epoxy based materials. Mold releases and accessory materials are also available from this manufacturer.

**Plastic Additives for Concrete**

Plastic fortified Portland cements and plasters also constitute excellent putties for use over wire screen armatures.

The Dewey and Almy Chemical Division of the W. R. Grace Company, Cambridge, Massachusetts, offers several synthetic additives for Portland cement. Among their products is: Super-Bondit, a latex additive for concrete, added to Portland cement in place of most of the mixing water. Because of its strength and adhesive characteristics, this additive lends itself admirably to build-up sculpture over armatures. Dura Weld, another product, is a vinyl acetate copolymer latex additive for concrete; used for making concrete stuccos or as a "plastic concrete" coating, it is mixed with about 50% water.

This company also distributes Thiopoxy 60 and 61 (modified epoxy compounds), which are plastic coatings for concrete, wood, and metal. Mixed with a hardener, Thiopoxy cures by catalytic action overnight to produce extremely hard surfaces. Tensile strengths of up to 10,300 PSI (as compared to 3,600 PSI for concrete) are typical of this material. Thiopoxy coatings provide excellent protection against impact, abrasion, and chemical corrosion.

**Construction** by Jimenez Botey, plastic wood over wooden armature. Commercially available synthetic wood putty was used to create surface texture over a wooden construction.

**Chromoglyph** by Nicholas Roukes, 2′ x 4′, aluminum epoxy over concrete. Plastic putty can be effectively built up over precut, precast, or modeled forms of another material.

**Eve and Adam** by Bert Schwartz, 2′ high, plastic aluminum over expanded metal.

**Performers** by St. Maur, 8″ high, thixotropic polyester paste over wire armatures.

# 10 Imbedding and Casting with Clear Polyester

Clear polyester resin has been used extensively for imbedding objects for preservation and for display. Craftsmen have used it for making jewelry; hobbyists have used it for making all types of novelty items.

To date, not much has been done with this material in sculpture, although there are easy techniques involving the encapsulation of various materials within the plastic. Casting large forms, however, is quite tricky due to excessive heat build-up during the polymerization cycle. Thicknesses over ½″ require very careful calculations for determining proportions of catalyst and resin in order to avoid fractures. Large castings are usually made by multiple pourings, which build up volumes composed of several strata.

**Imbedding Objects in Clear Polyester**

To make transparent plastic casts which include materials such as metal, thread, gemstones, coins, clock parts, and other found objects, the multiple pouring method is recommended. A mold — such as a shallow tray of plastic, glass, or ceramic — is first lightly waxed; then ¼″ of catalyzed clear polyester casting resin is poured into the mold and allowed to gel. A variety of collage materials may then be arranged over the gelled surface; additional catalyzed resin is then poured over it. The second pouring is also allowed to gel and the process of arranging additional objects can then be continued.

In this manner, many objects may be positioned carefully within the transparent space of the casting and intermediate transparent shapes and effects are achieved. Both transparent and translucent dyes are available to color the resin. (See Sources of Supplies.)

**Casting Three-Dimensional Forms with Clear Polyester**

Very little catalyst should be used in pouring voluminous castings more than 2″ thick. Peak exothermic temperatures may cause castings to smoke, crack, or shatter if too much catalyst is mixed with the resin. If possible, catalysts which develop low peak exothermic temperatures should be used.

The use of inclusions and fillers within the casting also tends to dissipate heat during curing, thereby preventing fracturing. French artist St. Maur has developed a technique for controlling the dissipation of gases and heat within the plastic as it undergoes polymerization; in this way, he manages to produce beautiful crackles within his polyester sculpture. St. Maur's method involves a technique of pouring catalyzed and pigmented polyester resin into prepared plaster molds which contain many vent tubes. Through experimentation, he has perfected a technique of plugging and unplugging the vents during the polymerization of the resin, thus controlling the escape of heat and gases, and in this way, controlling the internal fissuring of the hardening plastic.

The final castings may be polished mechanically or chemically. Mechanical polishing is best done by using fine waterproof carbide sandpaper. The sandpaper is periodically dampened with water, then rubbed briskly over the plastic surface. Buffing wheels charged with tripoli are then used to produce a higher polish. Finally, the casting is hand polished with a cloth saturated with a non-abrasive carnauba paste wax which will give it a brilliant sheen.

To obtain a brilliant surface by chemical means, a thin coat of heavily catalyzed polyester casting resin may be brushed over the entire surface of the sanded sculpture. This method produces an extremely high gloss surface without much physical effort, and is commonly referred to as "chemical polishing."

**A Lamination Technique with Polyester Resin**

Polyester panels are easily made in thicknesses varying from ⅛″ to 1″ or more. The process of lamination simply means sandwiching many layers of flat materials within polyester resin and reinforcing fibreglass mat, and compressing the various layers to form an integral bond. To create thick panels (1″ thick or more), both lamination and casting techniques are employed. A basic working process may be described as follows:

(1) Cover a plywood or Masonite work surface with Mylar (DuPont polyester sheeting) or other protective plastic sheeting.

(2) Wooden or aluminum strips (or self adhering sponge rubber weather stripping) are placed along the borders of the plastic sheeting to form a retaining frame. The metallic or wooden strips may be clamped to the surface with clothes pins, spring clips, or small C clamps. These should be lightly waxed to provide easy release.

(3) Cut a piece of fibreglass reinforcing mat (about 1 oz. weight) to fit within the frame and place it over the Mylar plastic sheeting.

(4) A quantity of catalyzed polyester casting resin is prepared, poured over the fibreglass mat, and smoothed out with a spatula or squeegee. The fibreglass mat, you will note, becomes transparent as it becomes saturated with the clear resin.

(5) Place various fabrics or other materials over the tacky resin. These may include any flat materials, such as cellophanes, printed materials, decorative and pierced papers, metallic foils, and a great variety of woven fabrics. Loose materials, such as metallic flakes, glass or plastic beads and pellets, may also be sprinkled into the lamination.

(6) An additional amount of clear polyester resin is catalyzed and poured over the work. This, in turn, is also spread out evenly with a spatula or

squeegee. The plastic resin may be tinted with dyes, or the dyes may be squirted over the work directly, and then manipulated with a stick to create a variety of swirls or other chromatic effects. Place an additional sheet of fibreglass reinforcing mat over the work, and saturate with catalyzed polyester resin. A sheet of Mylar plastic is then placed over the lamination and pressure is applied to the surface with the aid of a rubber roller or squeegee. This action will compress the laminate, and remove unwanted air bubbles.

(7) The Mylar plastic sheeting is removed after the resin has hardened. The process described above can be repeated until the desired thickness and effect has been produced by as many layers as you wish.

(8) When the final layer of polyester resin has been poured, a sheet of Mylar plastic is again placed over the top surface of the laminate, and pressure is again applied with the rubber roller or squeegee. This will produce a tack-free, glass-like surface on the laminated panel.

(9) After the resin has hardened, remove both sheets of Mylar plastic (front and back) and the retaining frame. The edges of the lamination are then trimmed and sanded.

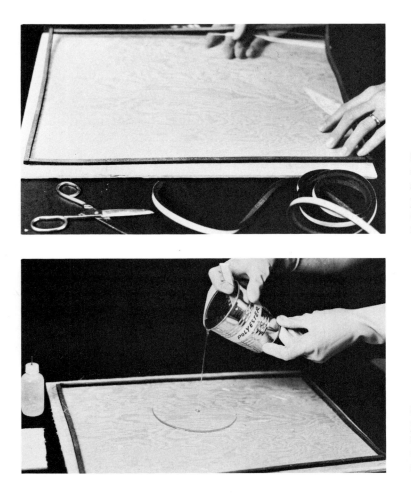

**Step 1:** The author begins a laminate of clear polyester casting resin. He first attaches sponge rubber weatherstripping to Mylar plastic sheeting. The self adhering weatherstripping makes an excellent retaining frame, resting on a sheet of plywood for rigidity.

**Step 2:** Catalyzed polyester casting resin is poured over the surface of the Mylar plastic sheeting. A cardboard squeegee is then used to spread the plastic resin evenly over the entire surface area.

**Step 3:** A sheet of reinforcing fibreglass mat is cut to size and placed over the wet surface of the plastic resin. Additional catalyzed polyester resin is poured over this surface and the squeegee is again used to distribute the resin. Fibreglass mat becomes transparent when impregnated with the casting resin.

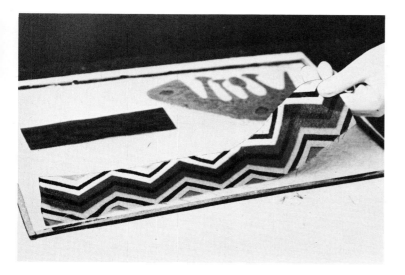

**Step 4:** Various flat materials are used to create the laminate. Woven materials, plastic theatrical spotlight gels, cellophanes, decorative papers, and other flat or loose materials are pressed into the wet resin. Materials are added until the desired effects are achieved.

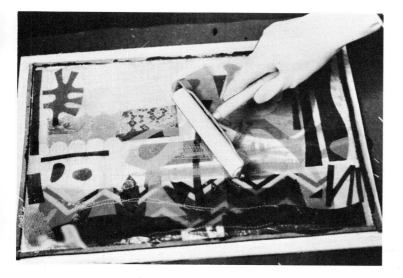

**Step 5:** Catalyzed polyester resin is poured over the work and spread evenly over the surface. A second sheet of fibreglass mat is placed over the wet surface and additional catalyzed resin is poured over it. A sheet of Mylar plastic sheeting is placed over the wet resin and a rubber roller is used to compress the laminate. This will remove air bubbles and insure a hard, glass-like surface.

# Casting a Figure with Clear Polyester

# 11

In this chapter, the author casts a torso of transparent polyester which contains fillers of broken glass and transparent dyes. The sculpture, *Xenia*, stands 16″ high and was cast in a plaster mold.

As can be seen from the color reproduction of *Xenia*, the chief advantage of working with clear polyester casting resin is the ability to produce transparent sculpture which captures and refracts light internally. Furthermore, by using pieces of broken glass and transparent polyester dyes in the inclusions, shimmering jewel-like qualities may be achieved in this type of casting.

**Modeling the Torso**

I used a standard approach in modeling this sculpture. Water based sculpture clay was modeled over an armature of metal pipe. The armature was similar to the one used for the sculptured head described in Chapter 7. Because the final casting was to be transparent and the internal character of the sculpture was to be complex, I designed the structural shape in simple, stylized volumes. Although there were both concave and convex forms, I purposely designed the clay sculpture to avoid undercuts.

In the beginning, a variety of wire loop tools was used to model the sculpture. Later, I used a flat kitchen knife edgewise to burnish the clay to a slick surface finish.

**Making the Mold**

The mold for this sculpture was made in two sections with plaster of Paris, applied in the same manner as described in Chapter 7. Shims of thin aluminum sheet were inserted into the clay model to divide the sculpture into two parts. Plaster of Paris was mixed and applied to create a mold thickness of approximately ¾″.

After the plaster had set, the two sections of the mold were removed and allowed to dry thoroughly for about a week.

**Preparing the Mold**

The bone dry mold sections were given three coats of clear lacquer to seal the porous plaster. These were followed by an application of paste wax mold

**Laminated Panel** by Nicholas Roukes, 12″ x 19″. Clear polyester casting resin and flat inclusions. The laminate cured in about an hour, after which time the two sheets of Mylar plastic sheeting and the sponge rubber retaining strips were removed. The work was allowed to cure overnight. The following day, the edges were sanded.

release, which was allowed to dry, then polished with a soft cloth. Waxing and polishing were repeated to obtain a slick mold surface. Finally, this surface was given two coats of PVA mold release, with a soft brush; the first coat dried thoroughly before the second was applied.

The two halves of the mold were fastened together with masking tape; the seams were sealed by pressing plasticine into the crevices. The mold was then placed in a cardboard box in an inverted position.

**Casting with Clear Polyester**

In preparing to cast *Xenia,* I filled the mold with broken, irregular fragments of clear bottle glass. Before the clear catalyzed resin was poured into the mold, polyester dyes were dripped directly onto the glass in the mold, allowing the transparent color to cascade down over the glass fragments.

Most of the solid castings which are made of polyester are quite small in scale. The principal problem of casting this resin in solid volumes lies in controlling the severe exothermic heat which is produced during polymerization. This is controlled to some extent by using very small amounts of catalyst and allowing for longer periods of cure. I have also found that glass fillers absorb much of the exothermic heat and the basic problem is eased.

It is absolutely essential that the catalyst be mixed evenly throughout the polyester resin. Rather than mix a large or complete quantity at one time, I prepared small successive batches, poured them into the mold, and repeated the operation until the mold was filled.

It is almost impossible to give exact proportions for catalyst-resin combinations because many factors influence the cure. Some of these factors are: thickness of casting, type of catalyst used, whether or not a filler is used to absorb some of the exothermic heat, and room temperature. However, here is a general guide which the sculptor may use as a point of departure. The following are suggested resin-catalyst combinations for clear polyester resin and MEK peroxide catalyst. ⅛″ thick, 15 drops of catalyst; ½″ thick, 8 drops; 1″ thick, 6 drops; 6″ thick, 2 drops.

**Steps in Casting**

In casting *Xenia,* which measures about 16″ x 4½″, 12 ounce batches of catalyzed resin were mixed and poured successively until the mold was filled. Two drops of catalyst were used per ounce of resin. Each catalyst-resin batch was stirred for about two minutes before it was poured. Curing took place over a period of 24 hours at a room temperature of 72°F. Between pourings of the catalyzed resin, additional polyester dye was dripped into the mold.

**Removing and Finishing the Casting**

After 24 hours, I gently pried apart the two halves of the mold with a spatula and removed the casting. Since polyester resin shrinks to a small degree, it was quite easy to remove the casting. To remove and polish the seam areas, I used both coarse and fine carbide sandpaper. Additional surface sanding was done with fine wet-dry carbide paper, with water as a lubricant. An extremely slick surface was produced. For a high gloss finish, heavily catalyzed polyester casting resin was brushed over the surface of the torso.

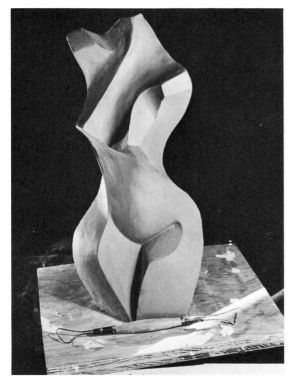

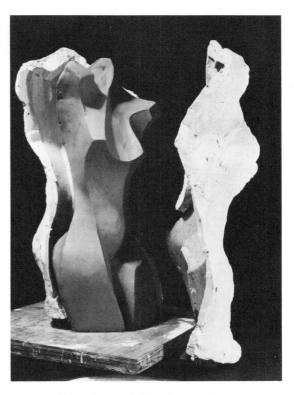

**Step 1:** Pugged water based sculpture clay is used to model the sculpture, *Xenia*. The sculptor uses a simple, stylized structure of convex and concave forms.

**Step 2:** The plaster mold is designed in two parts, containing no undercuts, and is approximately ¾" thick. The mold is allowed to dry thoroughly and the insides are then treated with lacquer, wax, and PVA mold release.

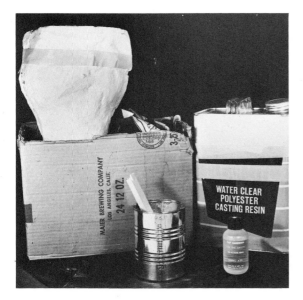

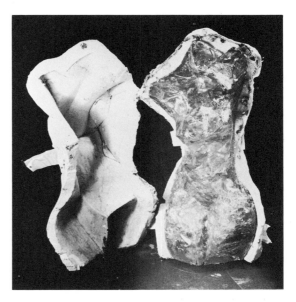

**Step 3:** The two sections of the mold are assembled and inverted in a cardboard box. Broken bottle glass is used to fill the mold, and transparent polyester dyes are dripped over the fragments. Small successive quantities of clear catalyzed polyester resin are poured into the mold until it is filled. Approximately 24 hours are allowed for curing.

**Step 4:** Now the mold is parted to reveal the transparent polyester casting. The slight shrinkage of the polyester resin facilitates removal of the casting. Wet-dry carbide paper is used to refine the seams and surface blemishes on the sculpture.

**Xenia** by Nicholas Roukes, 16″ high, transparent polyester resin with dyes and inclusions. Light is trapped and refracted within the interior of the sculpture, producing a brilliant interior radiance. A final polish is created by brushing the surface of the sculpture with highly catalyzed polyester resin, which produces a brilliant, transparent surface. (See plate in color section.)

# Impregnating Porous Materials with Polyester 12

Porous materials such as fabric, wood, plaster, and concrete may be coated with polyester for the following effects: surface coating; bonding or adhering; creating rigid forms from flexible materials.

Robert Mallary of New York has worked with cloth and polyester for many years, dipping and saturating a variety of fabrics, including clothing, into catalyzed polyester and shaping the material while the plastic hardens. Tuxedos become rock hard objects; flexible fishnets become rigid.

Two principal methods may be employed to impregnate materials:

Polyester resin, properly catalyzed, may be poured into a pan or bowl. Materials may then be immersed in the plastic resin, saturated, arranged in the desired shape, and allowed to harden. Protective gloves should be worn, and safety precautions, such as proper ventilation, should also be considered. The saturated cloth may also be draped over armatures and manipulated to model specific shapes and forms.

In the alternative method, fabrics and other materials are arranged first, then painted with catalyzed polyester resin. In this case, several coats of resin are applied over the assemblage. Textural surfaces may also be created by sprinkling sand, marble dust, or other loose materials onto the wet resin before the plastic hardens. Burlap, canvas, leather, cardboard, wood, sponges, papers, and other porous materials may be used in this technique.

**Two Impregnating Methods**

Catalyzed polyester may readily be used as a surface coating, either as a "paint" or as a plastic "varnish." Thinned slightly with styrene monomer, it adheres solidly to porous material, penetrates the material, and gives excellent protection against weathering, chemicals, etc. It is commonly used by the furniture industry for this purpose. The resin gives the original materials greater strength and makes them waterproof.

Sculptures of wood, plaster, and concrete may be coated with polyester for this purpose. Over wood, the catalyzed polyester bonds permanently and reveals the rich quality of wood grain in a highly lustrous surface which rivals the finest of finishes.

Furane Plastics, 4516 Brazil Street, Los Angeles, California, manufactures and distributes Plaspreg, a plastic impregnant for plaster castings. The Cal Resin Company, 14812 Raymer Street, Van Nuys, California, also supplies a variety of impregnating plastic resins. Detailed information regarding these products may be obtained by writing directly to the manufacturer.

**Polyester as a Surface Coating**

**Impregnating and Draping Fibreglass Cloth**

A unique method of creating three-dimensional sculpture of polyester resin involves coating fibreglass cloth with catalyzed resin, draping the cloth over prepared forms, then allowing it to harden into a rigid shell. By repeating this operation, the sculptor can make many component sections of a sculpture. The rigid forms are later joined together to complete the sculpture. The general working process may involve the following steps:

(1) A piece of plywood or Masonite is used as a work surface. This should be covered with Mylar plastic sheeting or some other protective plastic material.

(2) A piece of heavyweight fibreglass cloth is placed over the work surface.

(3) An appropriate amount of catalyzed polyester resin is prepared and brushed over the fibreglass cloth.

(4) The cloth is then picked up and draped over previously prepared forms, or suspended by string at various points, allowing the fibreglass to sag into interesting shapes. Forms of wadded paper, wood, plaster, polyurethane, metal, stone, or other material may be used to drape and shape the resin impregnated fibreglass cloth. As the tacky cloth will stick to practically anything it touches, the hump molds and forms should be isolated with a parting wax or cellophane film. The impregnated fibreglass cloth is then allowed to harden while draped over the hump forms. Protective gloves should be used in handling the tacky cloth, and the work should be carried out in a well ventilated area.

(5) Another section of fibreglass cloth is cut and placed on a second sheet of Mylar plastic sheeting, then coated with catalyzed resin and the process repeated to create as many rigid shells as are required for the sculpture.

(6) The rigid component shells are joined together by applying an appropriate amount of catalyzed polyester paste resin to the edges, then pressing the sections together and allowing the resin to harden. Tape or small C clamps may be used to hold the sections temporarily while the resin hardens.

(7) The completed sculpture may be given a final surface coating of pigmented catalyzed polyester resin, or may be textured by painting the surface of the sculpture with catalyzed resin and then sprinkling fine marble dust or other fillers over the tacky surface.

**Step 1:** In beginning this sculpture, the author cuts a variety of three-dimensional shapes from rigid polyurethane slabs and arranges them over a work surface of Mylar plastic sheeting. Liquid wax is brushed over the polyurethane forms as a release agent.

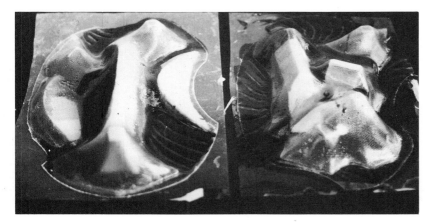

**Step 2:** Heavyweight fibreglass cloth is draped over the polyurethane forms and arranged to create a sculptural relief. The cloth is then impregnated with catalyzed polyester casting resin, applied directly to the fibreglass cloth with a 3″ household paint brush. Enough catalyst was added to the polyester resin to harden it within one hour.

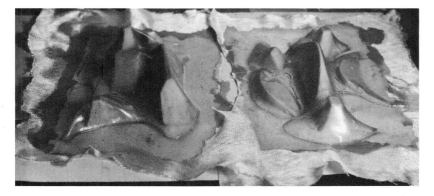

**Step 3:** After the resin hardens, both shells are trimmed (to match one another's shapes) with a pair of metal shears. The interior polyurethane cores are removed and the two shells are replaced on the surface of the Mylar sheeting for further work. Small quantities of catalyzed casting resin are poured into paper cups; transparent dye or pigment is added, creating a "palette" of plastic colors, applied to the shells with a brush, an eyedropper, or by dripping. The shells are then allowed to cure overnight.

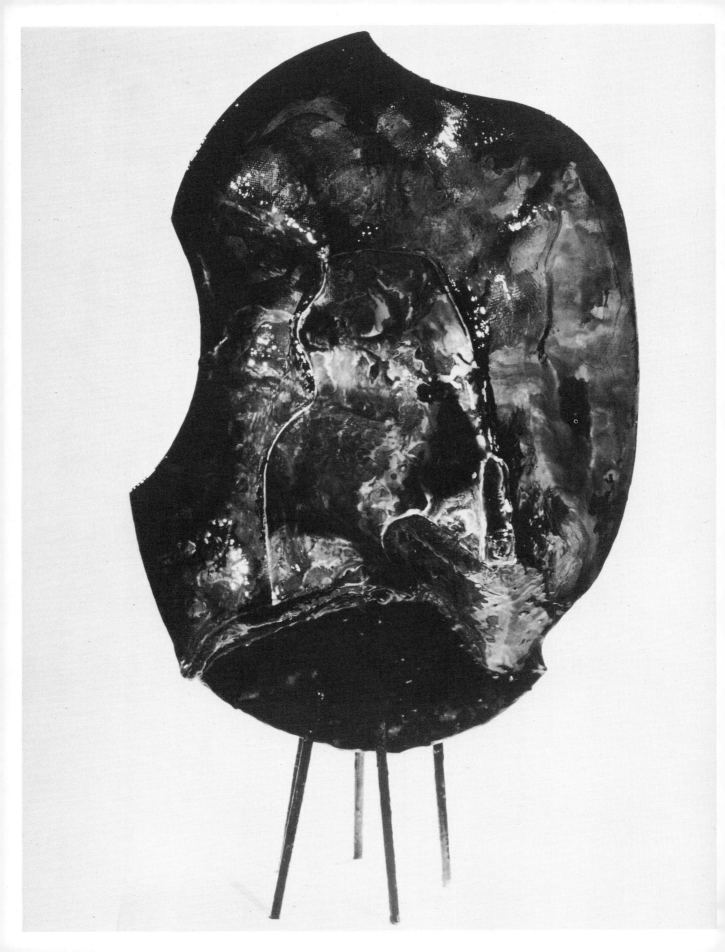

**Sculpture** (left) by Nicholas Roukes, fibreglass cloth impregnated with polyester. The two shells are attached to each other with catalyzed polyester resin. Seams are refined by filing and sanding, and are later painted with clear resin, heavily catalyzed. The completed sculpture possesses brilliant, transparent, translucent, and opaque color. It is mounted over a wooden base, using ¼″ metal rods. (See plate in color section.)

**Crucifix** (above left) by Robert Mallary, 7′ high, polyester saturated clothing, Houston Museum, photograph courtesy Allan Stone Galleries, New York. Old clothes were carefully draped and rigidified with catalyzed liquid polyester.

**The Fisherman** (above right) by Robert Mallary, 7½′ high, polyester impregnated wood and fishnet, courtesy Allan Stone Galleries, New York. Here polyester acts to integrate and preserve found objects and rigidifies even an intricate, fragile net.

# 13 Epoxy Resins

Sculptors will find that the handling characteristics of the epoxy resins are somewhat similar to the characteristics of polyesters. Epoxy resins, however, are favored by some artists for a few special characteristics which polyesters do not possess.

**Characteristics of Epoxies**

Epoxies are tougher; some offer tensile strengths up to 65,000 PSI. They have greater impact and compressive strength than the polyesters, and will stick to virtually any non-greasy surface. Because of their adhesive properties, they are excellent bonding agents for metal to metal, as well as for assemblages of mixed materials.

These liquid, straw colored resins offer very low shrinkage during curing and are dimensionally stable, once hardened. Like the polyesters, they are cured at room temperature by the addition of a curing agent or hardener, and are considered lightweight sculpture materials. They may be filled with pigments, dyes, or other fillers.

The Dow Chemical Company, one of the major producers of epoxy resins, has created over 30 varieties of epoxies to satisfy industrial demands. Union Carbide reports that their Bakelite epoxy based adhesives often provide bonds stronger than metals. Epoxy resins offer virtually no volatile loss during curing and exhibit extremely high solvent resistance and chemical resistance. Some of the resins are impervious even to hot caustics and acetone. The electronics industry favors epoxy resins for encapsulating delicate electronic components because the resins offer a chemical inertness which does not adversely affect inclusions within the material.

The epoxy resins are relatively new to the plastics field, having been introduced in the late 1940's. As surface coating, they have provided some of the toughest paint films yet produced. As adhesive putties, they have revolutionized the automotive body repair business. As an inert encapsulating and potting material, they are unequalled.

**Disadvantages**

A chief disadvantage of using epoxy resins is cost; they tend to be more expensive than polyester resins.

Like polyester resins, epoxies should be treated as potentially hazardous materials. Safety and hygienic rules should be observed and manufacturers' recommendations and instructions should be strictly observed. Skin contact should be avoided, and disposable mixing sticks, gloves, and mixing containers should be used. These resins have been known to cause skin irritations. The curing agents and accessory chemicals should be handled with extreme care as they can cause serious burns or irritation to the skin.

Well ventilated working areas should always be provided.

There are two principal classes of epoxy resins: liquid state and solid state. The liquid resins are converted to solids by the addition of a hardener, such as amine or acid anhydride. Many of the methods employed in handling polyester can be used. Lay-ups with fibreglass, casting, impregnation, bonding, or direct build-up techniques are readily done.

(1) *Bonding:* Epoxy adhesives are available in dual packages, one containing formulated resin and the other containing curing agent. These resins produce extremely tough bonds for practically all materials.

(2) *Reinforced plastic sculpture:* Epoxy resins are capable of making extremely strong fibreglass laminations, possessing very low shrinkage during the curing cycle. Catalyzed liquid epoxy is used for making lay-ups with fibreglass cloth or matting.

(3) *Surface coatings:* Epoxy resins may be applied to virtually all non-greasy surfaces of wood, metal, plastic, glass, etc. Epoxy bonds well with dissimilar materials and produces tough surface coatings. Epoxy is easily pigmented or filled. Two-system epoxy paints (like the two-system adhesives above) are commercially available from most paint stores; these are among the most permanent and durable paint films produced.

(4) *Molding compounds:* Epoxy resin may be filled with silica flour, asbestos, talc, sawdust or wood flour, chopped fibre, powdered or sintered metals, and mineral powders and granules. Many putties are commercially prepared as automotive body pastes and are readily available at automotive supply stores. Epoxy putties are excellent materials for use with direct build-up techniques over metal screen or wire armatures.

The French sculptor Gerard Singer uses epoxy resin in a very unusual way. His technique consists of first carving and texturing Styrofoam plastic, creating a bas-relief. He carves the sculpture quickly by using an electric drill equipped with sanding and routing bits. He also textures the material by igniting and extinguishing the Styrofoam with a propane torch.

Epoxy resin is then applied to the styrofoam surface with a brush, building up thicknesses of ¼″ to ½″. When the resin has hardened, lacquer thinner or acetone is applied to the Styrofoam, dissolving it completely, and revealing the epoxy bas-relief. The epoxy is unaffected by the thinner.

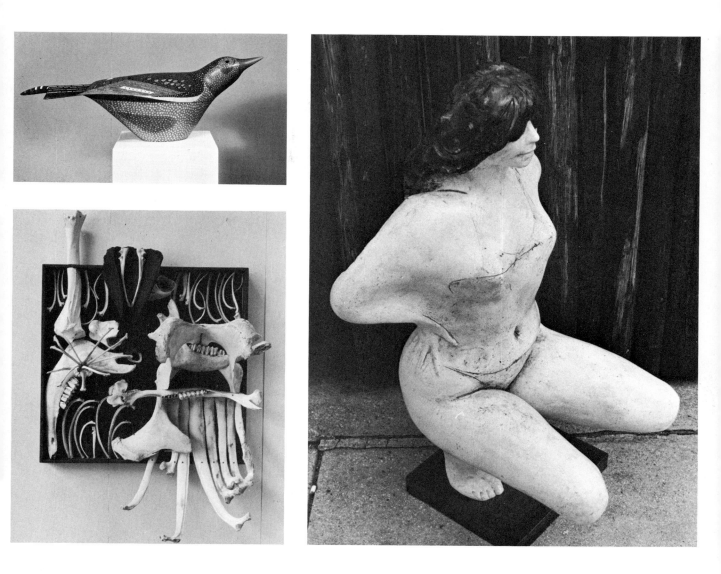

**Standing Beach Figure** (left) (detail) by Frank Gallo, 63″ x 18″ x 11″, epoxy, photo courtesy Graham Gallery, New York. This plastic cast retains the character of the clay original — note the hair texture — but is subtly treated with color.

**Finch** (upper left) by Emile Norman, 15″ high, epoxy, wood, and ivory, Morisey & Bengtson Collection, Big Sur. This artist applies a layer of epoxy, wood, and ivory tesserae over a wax form — which is then melted away, leaving an epoxy and wood shell.

**Bones** (lower left) by Robert McChesney, 40″ x 28″, epoxy and bones. The adhesive qualities of epoxy paste were used to attach these found objects to a wooden surface.

**Knee Bend Figure** (above right) by Frank Gallo, 30″ x 18″ x 17″, epoxy, photo courtesy Graham Gallery, New York. Although cast from a clay original, this figure explores the smooth, luxurious surface of the plastic to achieve the tactile quality of flesh.

# 14 Acrylic Sheet

Sometimes cast acrylic sheets are called *plastic glass,* owing to their outstanding optical characteristics. These thermoplastic resins are transparent or translucent; they offer over 90% light transmission and are used in optical products, such as lenses in eyeglasses and cameras. Their most common application, however, is for aircraft windows and domes, room divider panels, lighting fixtures, window panes, automobile tail lights, food containers, and advertising signs and displays.

**Properties of Acrylic Resins**

The acrylics are resins of methyl methacrylate and chemically related polymers which were developed in the early 1930's. They are approximately half as heavy as glass of comparable cast thickness and size, and are much stronger than glass in impact resistance. Tests have shown that acrylic sheets possess 6-17 times the impact resistance of double strength glass. A disadvantage, however, is that the acrylic surface is softer than glass, and must be protected from surface abrasion.

The acrylic resins are notable for their freedom from shrinkage and deterioration; they are only slightly affected by water, moisture, and general exposure. They are also fairly resistant to corrosion from most household chemicals, including many alkalis and non-oxidizing acids; but acrylics are attacked by the lower alcohols and aromatic solvents, such as turpentine, benzene, toluene, lacquer thinner, acetone, and ketones.

Principal manufacturers of acrylics in the United States are the Rohm and Haas Company, which makes Plexiglas; the American Cyanamid Company, manufacturers of Acrylite; and the DuPont Company, which manufactures the resins for Lucite. Perspex is a British acrylic, made by Imperial Chemical Industries. Altuglas is made by Altulor of France. There are several other manufacturers and the list is growing annually.

Acrylic resins are available in two forms: liquids (liquid monomers, emulsions, and syrups) and solids (powders, beads, sheets, blocks, tubes, and rods).

The liquid acrylics in emulsion form have revolutionized the paint industry and are responsible for exciting new artists' media. Uses of synthetic media

**Standing Girl** (right) by Frank Gallo, 70″ high, epoxy, courtesy Graham Gallery, New York. This artist models his figures in clay, casts them in epoxy resin which is then colored, polished, and textured. In this figure, the polished ivory finish of the flesh contrasts with the cloth-like texture of the dress .

**Assemblage #9** (left) by Nicholas Roukes, 36″ x 24″, polyester and mixed media. Various fabrics, leather, cardboard, and wood sections were attached with white glue and staples. Several coats of catalyzed polyester resin were then painted on and sand was sprinkled over the wet surface. When dry, the surface was painted with acrylic artists' colors. (See Chapter 12.)

**The Tomb** (above) by St. Maur, 14″ high, polyester. The artist applied colored polyester putty over a structure of wire mesh. (See Chapter 8.)

**Sixteen Light Musical Rectangles** (above) by John Van Saun, 67″ x 57″ x 57″, acrylic sheet, courtesy Howard Wise Gallery, New York. Boxes made of acrylic sheet contain lights of various colors. At the sound of chimes, the lights change, thus altering the colors of the boxes.

**Xenia** (right) by Nicholas Roukes, 16″ high, transparent polyester with dyes and inclusions. The figure was modeled in clay, then cast with the inclusions and dyes. (See Chapter 11.)

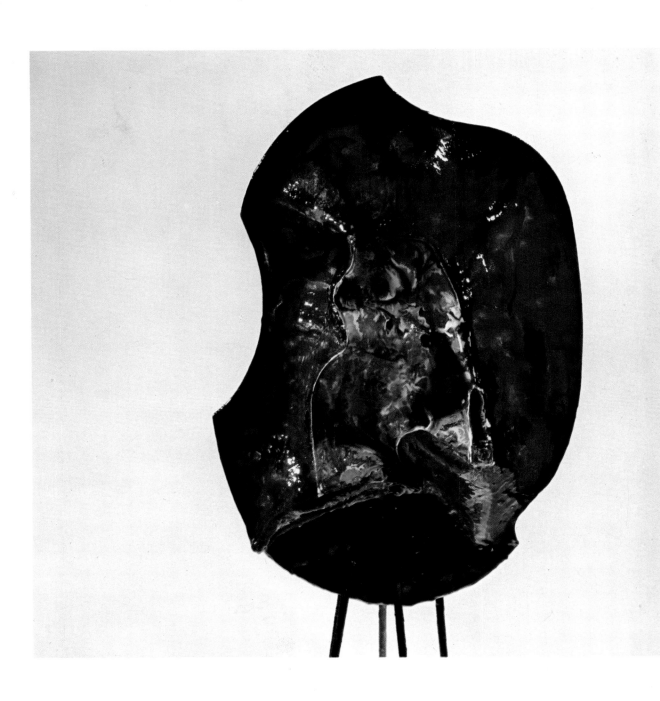

**Lighting Fixture** (detail) (left) by Sarah Reid, acrylic, Conrad Hilton Hotel, San Francisco. These cast methyl methacrylate monomer elements literally pipe the light outward from a central source.

**Sculpture** (above) by Nicholas Roukes is made of two shells, attached together like the halves of a clam, each of laminated fibreglass and polyester resin, colored with dyes and finished with a coat of clear resin. (See Chapter 12.)

**Requiem** (left) by Jonathan Batchelor, 18″ high, polyester and bronze powder. First modeled in clay, the figure was cast in a mixture of liquid polyester and bronze powder. (See Chapter 6.)

**Transparent Polychromed Panel** (above) by Claude Blin, 2′ x 2′, acrylic monomer and dyes on acrylic sheet. Various mixtures of liquid acrylic monomer and coloring agents are manipulated on a sheet of clear acrylic to produce an effect similar to stained glass. (See Chapter 15.)

**Evolution of Government** (above) by Albert Vrana, 16' x 550', cast concrete from polystyrene molds. This architectural wall at the Federal Office Building, Jacksonville, Florida, was cast in concrete from molds originally carved in plastic foam. (See Chapter 18.)

**Kathleen** (right) by Nicholas Roukes, life size, polyester. The head was modeled in clay, then cast in translucent polyester in a traditional waste mold. (See Chapter 7.)

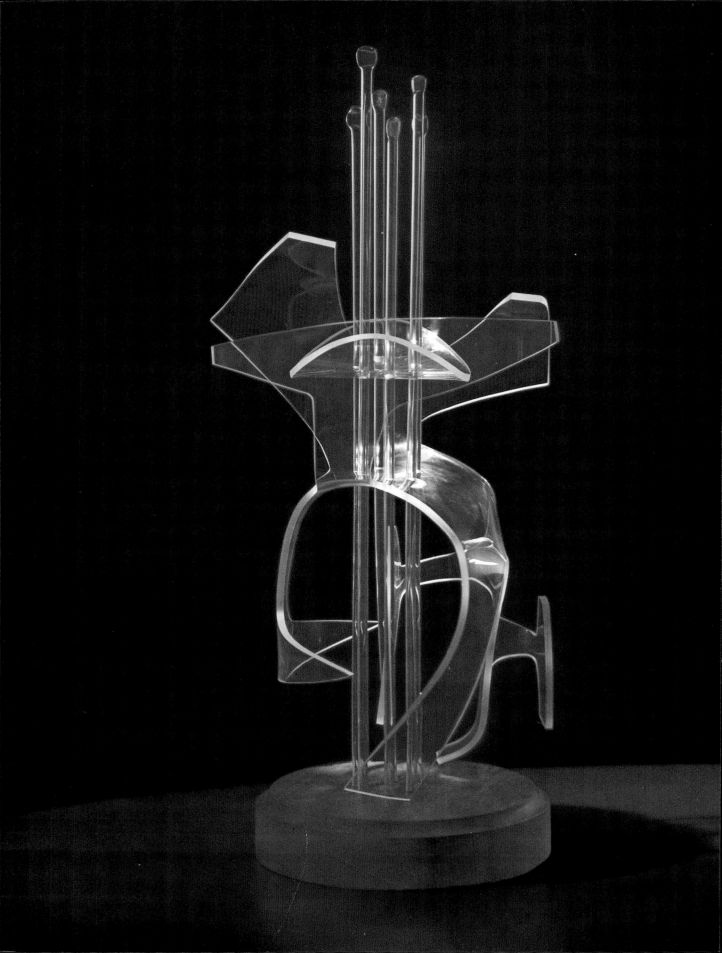

**Neos** (left) by Nicholas Roukes, 9″ x 24″, acrylic. Acrylic sheet and rods were cut and manipulated after softening with heat, then assembled with ethylene dichloride. The clear material absorbs and refracts light. (See Chapter 16.)

**Star Tree** (detail) (above) by Preston McClanahan, 62″ high, 96″ long, acrylic, courtesy Howard Wise Gallery, New York. Acrylic rods are clustered around a fluorescent light source, conducting light outward.

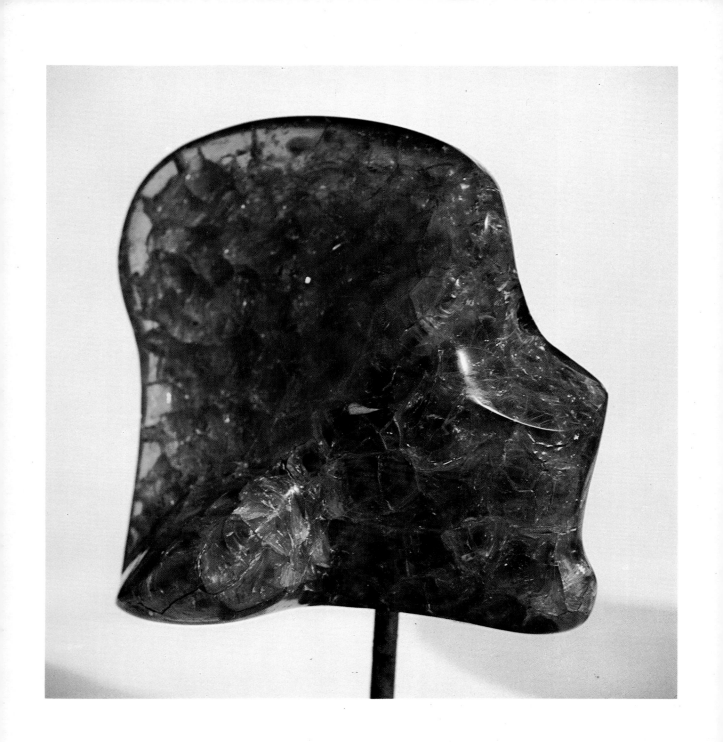

**Head** (above) by St. Maur, life size, polyester. Liquid polyester was cast into a plaster mold. The internal crackle was created by controlling exothermic heat during polymerization.

**Quiet Nude** (right) by Frank Gallo, 30″ high, epoxy, courtesy Graham Gallery, New York. The subtle use of color in this epoxy cast creates a remarkably lifelike skin tone.

in painting have been explored in a previous book, *Painting with Acrylics*, by this author and José Gutiérrez, published in 1965 by Watson-Guptill.

Although some sculptors have experimented with liquid acrylic monomers, special care and equipment is required, and the cost factor rules out this material for general studio practice. Most acrylic sculpture is made of solid sheets, blocks, tubes, and rods. These materials are easily worked with ordinary shop tools in the artist's studio.

Acrylic sheets are produced by mixing clear liquid monomers in various proportions. These polymerize to a hard, transparent solid. Polymerization is generally affected by the use of catalysts such as acid or ether peroxides, or diazo compounds, plus the addition of heat and pressure. The acrylic sheets are cast by pouring thick acrylic casting syrup between parallel sheets of plate glass. Colored sheets have dyes or pigments added to the casting monomer.

**Manufacturing Cast Acrylic Sheet**

In addition to many transparent, translucent, and opaque colors, acrylic sheets are also available in colorless clear and translucent forms, and in a variety of surface patterns and textures. Thickness of sheet material varies between $\frac{1}{16}''$ and $1''$. Rods and tubes are available in diameters of $\frac{1}{16}''$ to $18''$. Cast acrylic blocks are available in $5''$ to $12''$ thicknesses and dimensions up to $24'' \times 36''$.

Two types of acrylic sheets are manufactured: shrunk and unshrunk acrylic. The unshrunk acrylic will shrink approximately 2.2% in length, and will increase about 4% in thickness when heated for forming operations. The unshrunk material is less expensive, however, and because of this, is more desirable when heat forming operations are involved or when the shrinkage factor is of little concern.

The shrunk acrylic sheet is manufactured to exacting standards and tolerances, and remains a stable material throughout heat forming operations. This shrunk acrylic sheet has a higher standard of optical clarity. Acrylic sheet, such as Rohm and Haas' Plexiglas 1-A, is a grade of material which displays lower solvent resistance than other grades of Plexiglas sheet, making it ideal for solvent dyeing and laminating operations in sculpture.

An advantage of working with acrylic sheets is that ordinary shop tools and shop practices may be employed. With metal or woodworking tools and other common equipment, the materials are easily sawed, sanded, colored, heat formed, drilled, cemented, and polished.

**Working with Acrylic Sheets and Blocks**

**Chariot** (left) by Jacques Brown, 14′ high, polyester. Made of fibreglass and polyester over an armature of expanded metal mesh, this sculpture was designed for an experimental theater in Paris. The surface is animated by polyester pigments.

**Transferring Designs to Acrylic Sheets**

Designs and drawings are usually traced directly onto the protective paper which covers the plastic when it is delivered. This paper is allowed to remain on the surface of the soft plastic until all sawing and drilling operations are completed. Another way of applying a design is to rubber cement a cut paper pattern to the protective paper.

When sketching directly on the plastic surface, use a grease pencil, such as a China marking pencil. A soft cloth may be used to erase the drawing.

**Sawing Acrylic Sheets**

As mentioned before, any conventional woodworking or metal tools may be used when working with these plastics; this includes hand or power equipment. Blades designed for metal give the cleanest cuts. Although more expensive, special carbide tipped blades are available for cutting plastics, a table saw equipped with a fine toothed metal cutting blade is adequate for most cutting operations. The acrylic sheet should be fed slowly to avoid frictional heat build-up. Shop glasses should be worn for protection against irritating acrylic dust.

A blade recommended for cutting acrylic is a seven tooth per inch, 8″ diameter, hollow ground metal cutting blade, revolving at 1750 R.P.M. The blade should be set at a height approximately ¼″ above the plastic.

For cutting curved or intricate shapes, an electric jig saw is the most useful tool. Again, use a metal cutting blade, and feed it slowly to avoid gumming or re-fusing the acrylic through excessive heat build-up.

**Machining Acrylic Sheets or Blocks**

Machine tools such as lathes, shapers, routers, milling machines, drills, taps, etc., may be employed with acrylic sheets or blocks. Hand tools should be used on smaller pieces. In drilling or tapping operations, soapy water acts as an excellent lubricant.

**Sanding and Polishing**

Garnet or aluminum oxide abrasive papers give the best results in sanding operations. The work should progress from coarse to smooth sanding, as in woodworking. Grits 80-150 are typically used for rough sanding; 180-220 for smooth sanding; and 320-400 for final surface sanding. Wet sanding gives the best results.

**Buffing and Polishing**

In using double shaft electric buffing machines, one buffer should be charged with white tripoli compound for removing scratches, and the other with white acrylic polish compound for final gloss polishing. If a flexible shaft machine is used, two small buffs may be used interchangeably. Use light pressure to avoid burning the plastic. Final polishing should be done by hand, using a non-abrasive wax polish. Commercial plastic polishes, such as Meguiar's Mirror Glaze, are normally available from local boat or paint shops.

When attaching sections of acrylic sheet together, best results are obtained by using a solvent cement. First, be sure that both sections are smooth, clean, and well aligned. A solvent cement, such as ethylene dichloride, is applied to both surfaces with an eye dropper, a brush, or a hollow needle. (Other solvent cements include methylene dichloride and methyl methacrylate monomer.) The two sections of acrylic are softened by this solvent and a strong, transparent joint is effected. Strong, cohesive joints are made by allowing the solvent to soak into the plastic before light pressure is applied. Epoxy cements should be used in joining dissimilar materials to acrylic sheets.

**Cementing**

Annealing helps to reduce internal stresses created during machining or forming operations which use acrylic sheet. A project may be annealed by subjecting it to prolonged heat at elevated temperatures, followed by slow cooling. These temperatures are *under* the heat forming temperatures, 160°F.-230°F., and 2-24 hours. Recommended heating times for Plexiglas acrylic are listed below:

**Annealing Acrylic Sheets**

| Thickness (Inches) | Heating Time† in Hours for PLEXIGLAS Placed in a Forced-Circulation Air Oven Maintained at the Indicated Temperature | | | | |
|---|---|---|---|---|---|
| | 230°F.* | 210°F.* | 195°F.* | 175°F. | 160°F. |
| 0.060 to 0.150″ | 2 | 3 | 5 | 10 | 24 |
| 0.187 to 0.375″ | 2½ | 3½ | 5½ | 10½ | 24 |
| 0.500 to 0.750″ | 3 | 4 | 6 | 11 | 24 |
| 0.875 to 1.125″ | 3½ | 4½ | 6½ | 11½ | 24 |
| 1.250 to 1.500″ | 4 | 5 | 7 | 12 | 24 |

† Includes period of time required to bring part up to annealing temperature.

* Formed parts may show objectionable deformation when annealed at these temperatures. Use caution in annealing formed parts in the higher temperature ranges without testing.

Although annealing is desirable, it is generally inconvenient as studio practice — and not entirely necessary in most cases.

An undesirable accumulation of dust, caused by an excessive build-up of static electricity, may be checked by applying an anti-static coating to acrylic surfaces. The sculpture may be polished lightly between coatings. These coatings will prevent electrostatic charges for several months. (See "Sources of Supplies.")

**Anti-static Coating**

Avoid scouring powders and other abrasive types of cleaners when cleaning acrylic plastic. Only mild soap and water, applied with a soft cloth, should

**Cleaning Acrylic Plastic**

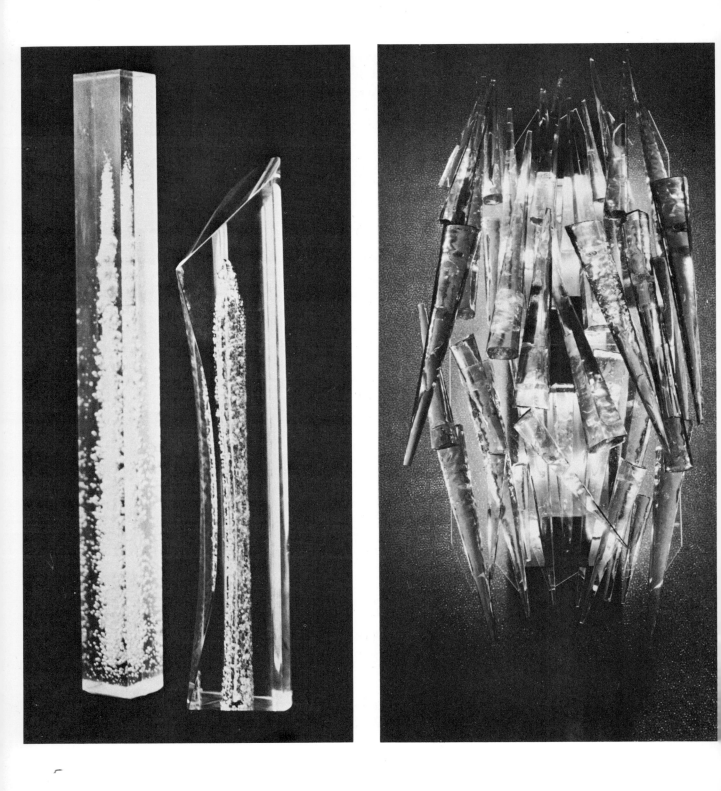

**Acrylic Sculptures** by Trevor Long, approximately 24″ high (left) and 18″ high (right). Cast methyl methacrylate monomer blocks contain internal bubbles created by the controlled exothermic heat reaction during polymerization of the acrylic resin.

**Lighting Fixture** (detail) by Sarah Reid, acrylic, Conrad Hilton Hotel, San Francisco. Cone shapes of cast methyl methacrylate monomer were assembled to produce "stalactite clusters" which act as brilliant refractors of light.

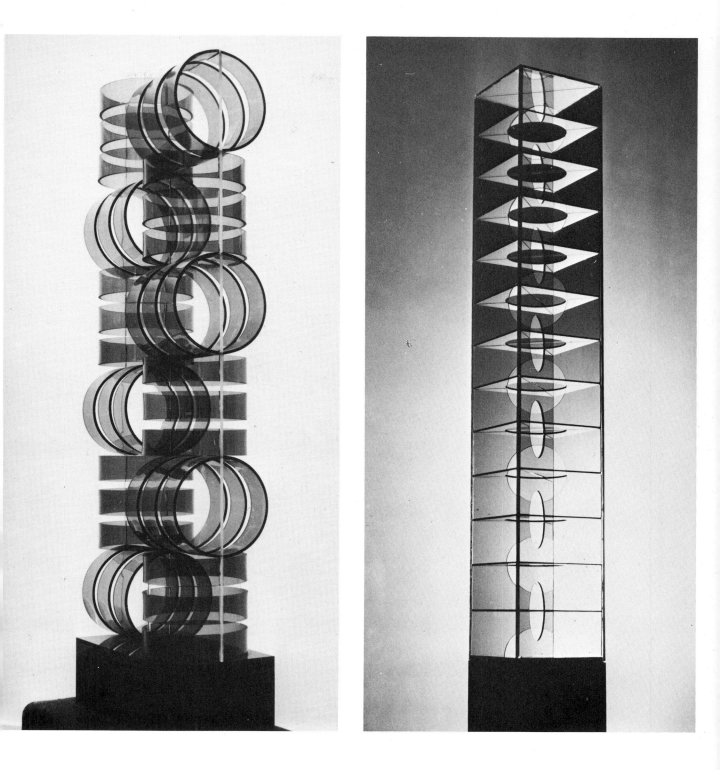

**Acrylic Construction** by Francisco Sobrino, transparent acrylic sheet. The artist exploited the transparency of the material to create an interplay of curving forms seen through one another.

**Interferences** by Francisco Sobrino, transparent acrylic sheet. This intricate optical design was developed entirely with rectangles and circles.

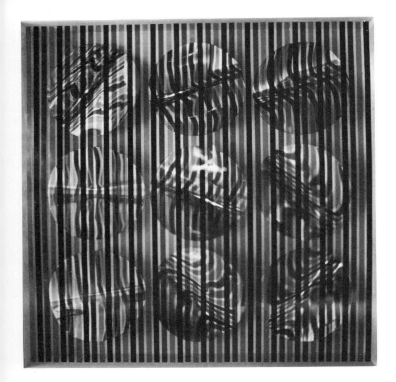

**Mobile Construction** (left) by Hugo DeMarco, clear acrylic sheet, green transparent acrylic strips, and aluminum. Nine reflectors of polished aluminum slowly move behind the transparent acrylic construction to create changing optical effects.

**Mobile Construction** (below) by Hugo DeMarco, acrylic. As the viewer moves, the circles are visually fractured by the triangles of acrylic sheet and new shape relationships are created.

be used. Do not use gasoline, alcohols, or typical window sprays, which will mar the surface. Many specially made plastic cleaners are available; apply these and polish with a soft flannel cloth.

Studio Methods with Acrylic Sheet

Although originally developed as a glass substitute, acrylic sheet is not glass, and should not be thought of as an inferior substitute for glass. Acrylic is a modern material with outstanding characteristics of its own, many of which are similar to glass, transparency in particular. Aside from light transmission and refraction, acrylic is easily formed into three-dimensional shapes, and may be used in a variety of ways. Among the many techniques which the artist may employ are the following:

(1) Heat forming
(2) Laminating
(3) Surface coating
(4) Three-dimensional construction
(5) Transparent collages, transparent mosaics, acrylic "stained glass"
(6) Engraving
(7) Prism structures
(8) Assemblage

Heat Forming Sculptures from Acrylic Sheet

The thermoplastic acrylic sheets will soften when heated to a temperature of about 250°F. At this stage, the plastic becomes soft and rubbery, and very pliable. It may be formed into a variety of three-dimensional shapes and allowed to cool to retain the new forms.

Commercial ovens, strip heaters, and vacuum presses are used by industry to shape the plastic into many complex shapes. The sculptor of limited means may use an ordinary kitchen stove, electric burner, or blowtorch to soften the acrylic sheet. Using protective gloves, the artist may hold the hot acrylic until it cools (after he has manipulated the material into a three-dimensional form).

At excessive temperatures, the plastic will burn and bubble, creating pitted surface textures; this could be an advantage, depending upon the artist's intention. Acrylic sheet will ignite at temperatures over 700°F. Unusual effects may be achieved by deliberately igniting and quenching flames. The first outstanding exponents of the art of heat forming acrylic sheet into transparent sculptures have been the famed experimenters Naum Gabo and Laszlo Moholy-Nagy, who pioneered transparent sculpture in the early forties.

Laminating Acrylic Sheet

Dramatic effects may be achieved by sandwiching acrylic plastic sheets together, using colored laminating cements. Panels for lighting fixtures, architectural windows, or three-dimensional constructions may be created in this manner. Colored laminating cements are usually made of high strength solvents, such as ethylene dichloride, methylene dichloride, or a mixture of both. (See Sources of Supplies for transparent dyes.) These laminating cements are commercially available in a wide color range of transparent colors, including fluorescent hues.

Generous amounts of laminating dye may be applied to the acrylic plastic sheet with eye droppers, spoons, or sticks, to create color patterns or other color effects. A second sheet of acrylic plastic is placed directly over the wet dye, and light pressure is applied. Internal textures are created by applying and relieving pressure on the acrylic sheets.

Loose materials, such as threads, metallic flakes, gold or silver leaf, colored threads, gels, cellophanes, foreign liquids, and other inclusions may be integrated into the "sandwich" for particular effects. Several sheets may be laminated together to build blocks of acrylic plastic which may later be carved, sanded, or machined.

## Surface Coating for Acrylic Sheets

Since color is an inherent characteristic of acrylic sheeting, it is not normally painted; however, in some cases, an artist may wish to coat acrylic surfaces for special effects.

Epoxy based paints create an excellent bond to acrylic surfaces. These paints are available in many colors and require an activator, which is mixed with the paints just prior to use. The pot life of the paints may be controlled to extend over a period of hours. These extremely durable paints are widely employed for marine and industrial uses.

## Transparent Colors

The Keystone Refining Company, 4821-31 Garden Street, Philadelphia, Pennsylvania 19137, manufactures and distributes Grip-Flex, an excellent transparent paint for acrylic and other plastics. This paint is available in a wide range of colors and is best applied by spraying. It may be purchased in 16 ounce aerosol spray cans. Also available is Grip-Mask, a sprayable masking agent for use with these paints.

Color pastes and liquids, dispersed in polyester, epoxy, or acrylic monomer resins, are available from manufacturers listed in "Sources of Supplies."

Polyester dyes can be obtained through craft and hobby shops that feature plastic resins. These dyes are readily dispersed in catalyzed polyester resin or in thixotropic polyester resin, and are used as transparent or translucent paints for acrylic sheet. Foreign materials, such as glass, may be pressed into the surface of the wet resin for additional interest.

## Dip-dyeing Acrylic

Transparent acrylic sheet or sculptured forms may be dyed either by immersing the plastic or by wiping it with special acrylic dip-dyes. The dyes, available from most plastic supply houses, are usually anilines dis-

**Cross** (left) by Robert Lepper, 26½″ x 10″ x 15″, acrylic. The sculptor has shaped and joined clear acrylic blocks.

**Freeform** (below) by Trevor Long, acrylic. A block of clear acrylic was drilled, routed, treated with dyes and pigments to produce a sculptural form containing a brilliant internal structure.

persed in a water-acetone base. The solid acrylic is either dipped or wiped until the desired transparent depth of color is achieved; then the plastic is rinsed with water and polished with a soft cloth.

**Three-Dimensional Constructions**

Many shapes of acrylic plastic, which have been sawed, sanded, and polished, may be joined with solvent cement such as ethylene dichloride. Acrylic forms may be constructed of thin or heavy stock, laminated sheets, or a combination of sheets, rods, and tubing, all of acrylic. Nylon fishing line may be used for linear effects.

**Transparent Collages and Mosaics**

To make a transparent collage or mosaic, glass tesserae and other loose materials are attached to a clear acrylic sheet with Duco all-purpose cement. Catalyzed clear polyester is then poured over the mosaic to bind the loose materials together to form a transparent mosaic.

**Acrylic "Stained Glass" Methods**

In making architectural panels, the artist may "draw" directly on the acrylic sheet with liquid aluminum, liquid steel, lacquer, or epoxy-aluminum filled pastes. Most of these pastes are available in tubes with long tips. The paste may be squeezed out to create raised line *cells,* similar to the leading of actual stained glass. The cells are then filled with catalyzed clear polyester, containing polyester dye or catalyzed acrylic monomer dyes. Brilliant architectural panels are possible with this technique. (See Chapter 15, "Making a Transparent, Polychromed Panel from Acrylic Sheet.")

Mylar plastic or cellophane should be used over the polyester-dye surface after it has gelled. Covering the surface overnight will exclude air and effect a harder surface cure of the polyester resin.

**Engraving Acrylic Sheets**

Intaglio designs are easily carved into acrylic sheets by using burr cutters mounted on flexible shaft tools. A sculptor may create surface designs which are later illuminated by edge lighting. Fluorescent lighting tubes, placed along the bottom or top edge of the acrylic plastic sheet, will "pipe" light along the interior surfaces of the plastic and out through the engraved design, providing brilliant illumination. Colored gels, mounted in front of the light source, may be used to color the light as it enters the plastic.

**Prism Structures of Acrylic Plastic**

Acrylic prisms are readily made by machining and polishing solid acrylic blocks. The prisms may be laminated together to form larger clusters, or bonded to the surface of an acrylic sheet, using a solvent cement such as ethylene dichloride. Infinite patterns of colors are produced by the juxtaposition of these clear prisms.

By applying generous amounts of catalyzed epoxy or thixotropic polyester paste to acrylic sheets, you can create a receptive ground for pressing and adhering a variety of loose materials and found objects. Stones, pebbles, mosaic tesserae, metal, or junk parts of mechanical objects may play a part in the construction of an assemblage.

Methyl methacrylate monomer is available from Rohm and Haas, DuPont, or Union Carbide Company. It is a thin, clear, volatile liquid which may be changed from a liquid monomer to a solid polymer by subjecting it to heat, light, or catalysts. The combination of heat and pressure is also used to polymerize (harden) acrylic monomer. Castings produced from acrylic monomer are crystal clear, with high optical quality; however, this material is not commonly used in studio practice because of complex handling demands.

Controlling the exothermic heat and internal bubbling caused by gases during polymerization are just a few of the problems to be met. For this purpose, many commercial firms use an autoclave — a device which controls both heat and pressure. With a very large casting, even an autoclave may not be adequate to control the exothermic reaction, and the casting may have to be made by multiple pours. Because methods of casting liquid monomers have not been simplified for studio use, this material is not recommended for general use by the artist.

Two bulletins which provide helpful information regarding monomer castings are: *Technical Bulletin No. X-28c: Lucite, Acrylic Resin-Embedment of Specimens,* published by DuPont; and a technical bulletin issued by Rohm and Haas entitled, *Embedding Specimens in Methacrylate Resins (SP-46).*

Transparent castings are more easily made with clear polyester casting resin, as outlined in Chapter 11, "Casting a Figure with Clear Polyester." Although not as optically clear as acrylic monomer, polyester resins are much more practical to handle for general studio use.

# 15 Making a Transparent, Polychromed Panel from Acrylic Sheet

In his studio near Paris, French artist Claude Blin uses an acrylic sheet and liquid dyes to produce a striking architectural panel. He describes his approach. . . .

The artist who designs transparent panels or walls must, of necessity, employ light as his principal means of expression. His work is, in a sense, a light trap which allows light to filter into and out of his creation. The work exists in both two and three dimensions — it is two-dimensional in its physical character, and three-dimensional in the *collage* of colored light it produces within a given space.

I have turned to plastic materials for making panels and windows for several reasons. Plastics are easy to handle, are weatherproof, and have impact resistance.

To create the panel which I will describe in this chapter, I used the following materials: (1) a clear, acrylic sheet measuring about 2′ x 2′ and ¼″ thick; (2) transparent dyes of primary and secondary hues, dispersed and catalyzed in methyl methacrylate acrylic monomer; (3) brushes, a palette knife, short wooden spatulas, and cardboard squeegees.

**Beginning the Transparent Panel**

To begin, I made several thumbnail sketches to visualize the general nature of my design. My intention, at this point, was to create a somewhat cellular motif which would offer opportunities to use brilliant dyes in its many areas. After developing the sketch, I made a full size drawing on a sheet of manila paper.

**Preparing the Acrylic Panel**

With fine carborundum paper, I sanded the surface of the acrylic sheet lightly to create a slight tooth which would facilitate the adhesion of the acrylic monomer dyes. The panel was then placed directly over the drawing and work was carried out on the horizontal acrylic sheet. (An even better solution would be to work on a light table; in this way, the artist can view the full effect of the transparent dyes as he applies them to the plastic panel.)

It should be noted that some surface tension is created on the acrylic panel as the resin-dyes polymerize. Therefore, to avoid warping, thicker panels should be used for large architectural works; or panels should be firmly set into wooden or metal frames before the work is begun.

At this stage, small quantities of acrylic monomer were poured into various containers, and small amounts of acrylic dyes were added to produce the desired hues. (See "Sources of Supplies.") As I began to work, I took a specific color, added the proper amount of catalyst, mixed it well, and applied the mixture to the panel with a brush, a stick, or a palette knife. The drawing, which was visible through the panel, was used as a guide as I began to describe the essential cellular forms of the design with a dark catalyzed resin-dye.

Resin-catalyst proportions were calculated to gel in about 15 minutes, so the work progressed swiftly. Some preliminary experimentation should be carried out with resin-dye proportions; some dyes have a definite inhibiting or accelerating effect on the catalyzed resin.

Additional colors were mixed, catalyzed, and applied to the interior areas of the cellular structure of my design. Many intense, transparent colors were employed; in some instances, the surfaces of the resin were *deliberately* disturbed as they began to gelatinize, thus creating interesting light refracting characteristics. Tools such as brushes, knives, sticks, and cardboard squeegees were used to manipulate the resin-dyes over the surface of the acrylic panel.

Curing took place at a normal room temperature of about 70°F., producing a fairly hard surface in about 30 minutes. Fifteen days, however, were allowed for complete polymerization.

It should be noted that the artist may substitute clear polyester resin, used with transparent dyes, to create transparent panels. To obtain a completely hard surface cure, a thin sheet of Mylar plastic should be placed over the gelled polyester surface to exclude air while curing.

**Preparing and Painting the Acrylic Panel**

**Step 1:** Preparing to create a transparent poly-chromed panel of acrylic plastic, Claude Blin makes a full size drawing from one of his preliminary thumbnail sketches.

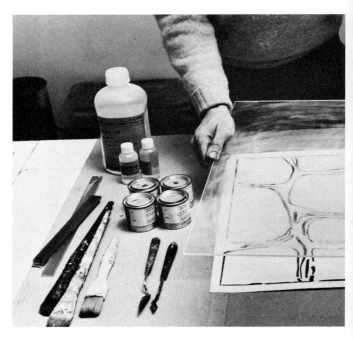

**Step 2:** Blin has lightly sanded the acrylic plastic sheet and now places it directly over the drawing. Seen to the left are tools and materials to be used: acrylic monomer and catalyst; cans of dyes; brushes, sticks, palette knives, and cardboard squeegees.

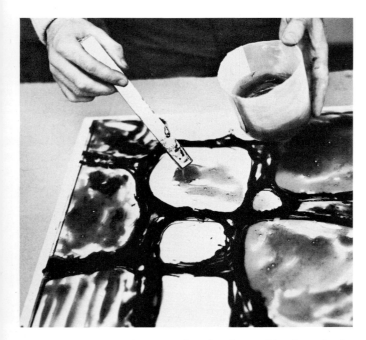

**Step 3:** Tracing the sketch, visible through the acrylic plastic sheet, the artist applies a dark cata-lyzed monomer dye to the plastic surface, develop-ing a cellular design motif. Other colored dyes are mixed with methyl methacrylate monomer, cata-lyzed, and applied within the cells of the design. Dyes are specially manufactured for plastic resin, and dissolve completely within the mixture to pro-duce brilliant, transparent colors.

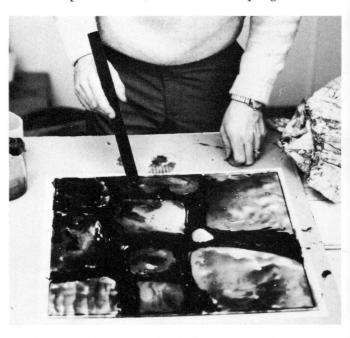

**Step 4:** Additional colored dyes are mixed, and the artist continues to develop the panel. The resin-dyes become gelatinous in approximately 15 min-utes, hard to the touch in about 30 minutes. Blin disturbs some of the gelatin surfaces to create more interesting light refracting qualities.

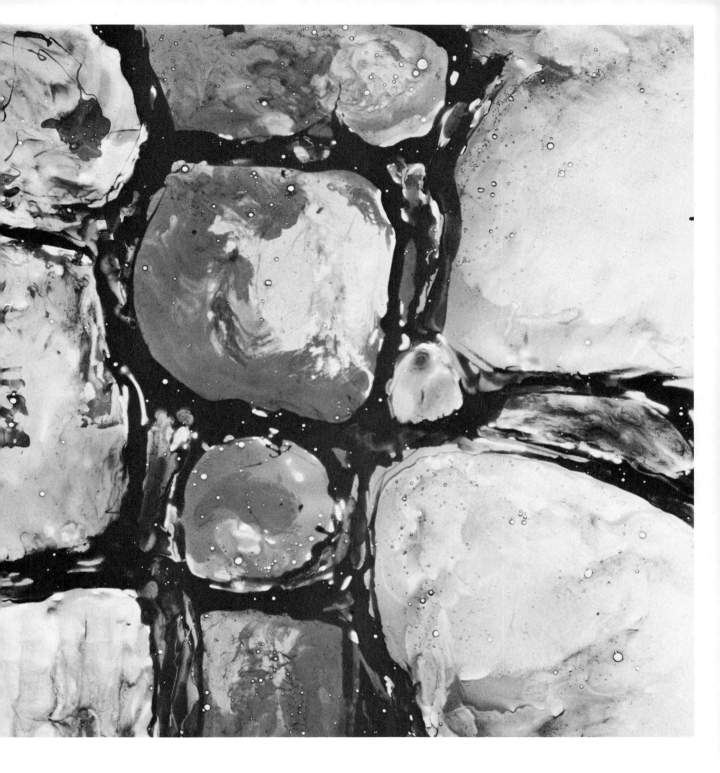

**Transparent Polychromed Panel** by Claude Blin, 2′ x 2′, acrylic. (See
plate in color section.)

# 16 Making a Sculpture from Acrylic Sheet

In this chapter, the author cuts and shapes flat acrylic sheet and extruded acrylic rods to form a three-dimensional sculpture entitled *Neos*. The completed sculpture measures 9″ x 24″.

Since World War I, sculptors have explored many materials. With the discovery of new materials came a new sculpture — transparent constructions containing a poetry inherent in the material itself. The early sculptures of Naum Gabo, for example, were beautiful prototypes of form and design, involving acrylic plastic and nylon cord. In their searching, a great number of other artists have discovered great possibilities in the use of these light-absorbing, light-refracting materials. Sculptors such as Laszlo Moholy-Nagy, Leo Amino, and Fred Dreher, have exploited the nature of acrylic plastics to produce outstanding work.

Transparent sculpture has been called by many names: light modulators, light compositions, prismatic sculpture, etc. However, whether he creates transparent sculpture or kinetic art, the contemporary artist will find tremendous possibilities in working with acrylics. The materials are now commonly available in sheet, rod, tube, or block form. They possess a crystal clear quality which refracts even more than glass, and they are easily cut and formed into complex forms and designs. Acrylic sheet is available from local plastic supply houses or directly from manufacturers such as Rohm and Haas (Plexiglas) and the Imperial Chemical Company (Perspex). Other manufacturers and distributors of acrylic materials are listed in this book under "Sources of Supplies."

In creating *Neos,* my initial aim was to make a sculpture which would be capable of accepting and *piping* environmental or designed lighting. I decided to develop the work spontaneously, beginning with a large form which was complex and biomorphic, and adding to it as I went along.

**Designing the Paper Pattern**

I began *Neos* by making several pencil sketches of free form shapes and selected the most interesting one for enlargement. As I made the two-dimensional designs, I tried to visualize the possibilities of bending these shapes into three-dimensional forms.

The full size ink drawing was carefully cut out with a pair of scissors and then attached to the surface of an acrylic sheet with rubber cement. The acrylic panel which I used was $\frac{3}{16}''$ thick and 20″ square. Thin paper was used to protect the soft acrylic sheet, and this paper was not removed until all cutting and sanding operations were completed.

An electric jig saw, equipped with a metal cutting blade, was used to saw the thermoplastic acrylic. I have discovered that it is a good idea to feed the plastic sheet *slowly* into the blade to avoid excessive heat build-up during sawing operations. A bar of soap makes an excellent lubricant for the saw blade.

After the acrylic sheet had been cut, a half-round file and medium grade carborundum paper were used to refine the edges of the plastic. High speed electric drills or Moto-Tools, equipped with miniature sanding drums, are excellent for refining the edges.

**Sawing the Acrylic Sheet**

Although commercially designed ovens are available for heating plastics, an electric oven or a burner on top of a stove will serve the purpose. Both paper pattern and protective paper were removed from the plastic cut-out shape and it was then placed in the oven. Temperature was set at 300°F. At about 250°F., the plastic becomes soft and pliable. At this point, it was removed from the oven and formed into a complex, three-dimensional shape. While I held the soft plastic in this new shape, an assistant cooled it with a damp sponge.

A few additional bends were necessary; I made these after softening selected areas of the plastic *over* (not on) one of the top burners of the electric stove.

**Heat Forming the Acrylic Plastic Sheet**

In the next operation, I decided to use several acrylic rods which were designed to run through the sculpture and provide support. I used a small 1/16″ drill bit (in an electric drill) to make preliminary pilot holes; I then drilled the final holes with a 1/4″ metal drill bit. The ends of the acrylic rods were softened over the electric burner and then squeezed with pliers to create flat shapes with rounded profiles.

In addition to the rods, I designed and made an oval form of acrylic plastic which constituted a third element for the sculpture. This form was also heated, bent slightly, and then drilled to accommodate the extruded rods.

**Drilling the Acrylic Plastic**

A circular wooden base was designed for the sculpture, and 1/4″ holes drilled into it to seat the acrylic rods. The three sections of the sculpture were assembled and final adjustments made; ethylene dichloride, applied with an eye dropper to the joints, made a permanent bond between the various elements of the sculpture.

A coat of anti-static wax was applied lightly over the surface, and the sculpture was finished with a light polishing.

**Assembling and Finishing**

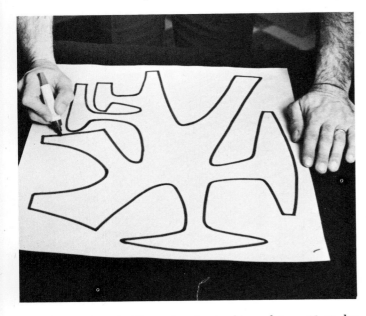

**Step 1:** The author begins his sculpture, *Neos*, by making several preliminary sketches. From these, a design is selected and enlarged to make a paper pattern, which he draws here in its final form.

**Step 2:** The paper pattern is cut out and attached to a ³⁄₁₆″ acrylic sheet with rubber cement. The thin protective cover sheet on the acrylic has not been removed.

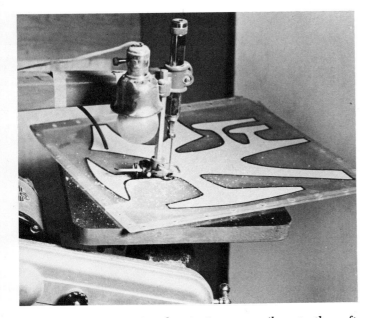

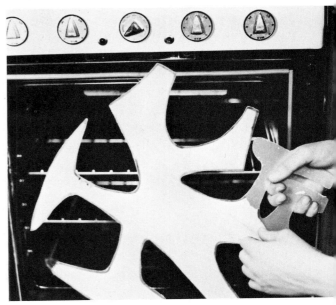

**Step 3:** An electric jig saw easily cuts the soft, thermoplastic material. The saw is fitted with a metal cutting blade and is occasionally lubricated with a bar of soap. The edges of the acrylic are refined with a half-round metal file and medium grit carborundum paper.

**Step 4:** Now the acrylic cut-out is stripped of paper and protective plastic in preparation for heating. An electric stove is used to soften the plastic. Oven controls are set at 300°F.

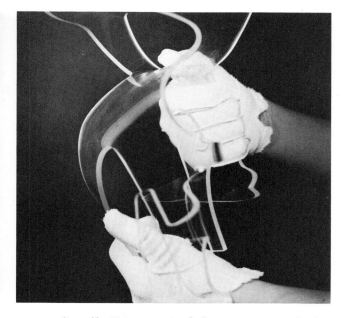

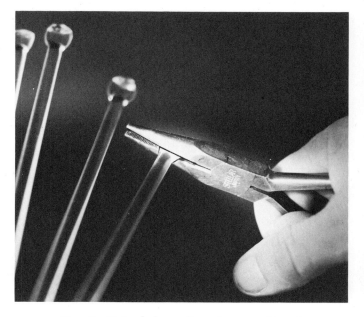

**Step 5:** Using a pair of gloves to remove the hot plastic from the oven, the artist easily forms it into various shapes. While the shape is held in this new position, an assistant cools and hardens the plastic with a damp sponge.

**Step 6:** Extruded acrylic rods are softened over an electric burner and squeezed with pliers to create flat ends with rounded profiles. The ¼″ rods will connect the two sections of the sculpture and support the work on a wooden base.

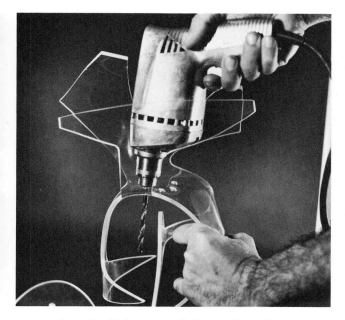

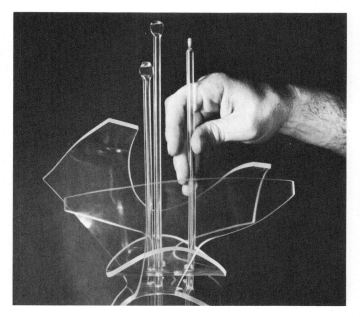

**Step 7:** Holes are drilled into the soft plastic to accommodate the acrylic rods. A high speed electric drill, equipped with a metal bit, is used to drill through the plastic. Pilot holes $\frac{1}{16}$″ in diameter were drilled first, then enlarged to $\frac{1}{4}$″ in diameter.

**Step 8:** The author assembles the sculpture, bonding the sections together with ethylene dichloride. The assembled sculpture is given a light coat of anti-static wax for a final surface polish and to prevent dust collection.

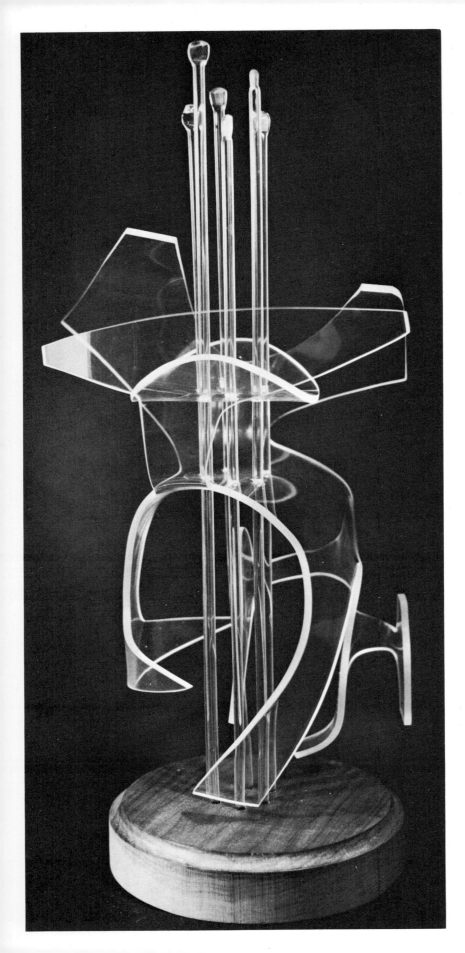

*Neos* by Nicholas Roukes, 9″ x 24″, acrylic. The crystal clear sculpture absorbs and refracts colored light, displaying an inherent characteristic of the acrylic material, methyl methacrylate. (See plate in color section.)

# Plastic Foams 17

Plastic foams are also called cellular plastics or expanded plastics. The materials are commonly used for boat flotation devices, for thermal and architectural insulation, for display and novelty fabrication, and as packaging material. They vary in density and are manufactured in both flexible and rigid forms. Flexible plastic foams, of course, have a long history as cushioning material for automobile seats and household furniture. Foamed plastics are available in two basic categories: solid and pour-in-place liquids. Solid foams are widely used by artists; liquids are rarely used because of their complexity and toxicity.

Solid foamed plastics are available in spongy or rigid varieties, with densities ranging from .1 to 60 pounds per cubic foot. Some of these densities are easily carved with a kitchen knife, while higher densities have a resistance typical of wood or stone, and require chisels for carving. These cellular materials are manufactured in slabs, blocks, logs, and a variety of extruded forms.

The lower density rigid foams, which are normally used for architectural insulation, are easily carved, but must be given a surface coating to make them more durable. Coatings such as polyester, epoxy, or modified concrete are generally used for this purpose.

**Properties of Foamed Plastics**

Most of the foamed plastics are white, beige, or light blue and are characterized by low thermal conductivity. They are dimensionally stable, fire resistant, and extremely lightweight. Most of the thermoplastic or thermosetting resins may be expanded to produce cellular plastics. Basic families of foamed plastics include materials made of: (1) cellulose acetate; (2) epoxies; (3) phenol-formaldehyde; (4) polyethylene; (5) polystyrene; (6) silicones; (7) urea-formaldehyds; (8) urethanes; (9) vinyls.

**Pour-in-Place Liquids**

Although liquid components are available for creating cellular plastics, they are not recommended for general studio use due to the extremely toxic nature of the chemicals. Furthermore, both chemicals and fumes are highly flammable. Proper studio facilities, including extractor devices for removing the corrosive fumes, are required. For this reason, not many sculptors use the liquid components, but prefer to work with the commercially available solid plastic slabs.

An exception is Roger Bolomey of New York, who works with liquid pour-in-place chemicals and has produced some outstanding work in this medium. His studio equipment includes an elaborate safety chamber and protective masks for use when he is working with these toxic chemicals.

**Manufacturing Plastic Foams**

Although the artist is not advised to undertake this process, the reader will be interested to know the several processes by which cellular plastics may be created: (1) by producing cases which are liberated within plastic mixes; (2) by using water or other liquids which are volatized within plastic mixes by heat or chemical reaction; (3) by the use of air, which is whipped into suspension within the plastic mix. In each case, the plastic mixture rises like cake batter, and is eventually polymerized to form a solid, cellular, substance.

A syntactic foam is produced by an entirely different process. Hollow beads of phenolic resin are mixed with catalyzed polyester, epoxy, or phenolic resin to form a thick batter of cellular plastic. Polystyrene is the most commonly used cellular plastic, manufactured under a variety of trade names. Styrofoam, created by the Dow Chemical Company, is one of the most commonly used.

**Studio Practices for Rigid Plastic Foams**

The artist will almost certainly buy ready-made blocks of foam from local building and plastic suppliers. The most practical materials are rigid polyurethane and polystyrene blocks. Methods of using these materials in the artist's studio vary; some are still highly experimental, while other techniques are well on their way toward becoming standard practices. Among the recommended and simpler techniques for using cellular plastics are:

(1) For direct carving.
(2) As a temporary mold making material for casting (see chapter 18).
(3) For assemblage and mosaics.
(4) For experimentation with solvents and light transmission.

**Working with Styrofoam**

Styrofoam is a trade name for Dow Chemical Company's polystyrene product. This material, which is made of polystyrene expanded approximately 40 times, will last almost indefinitely when protected from abrasion and from direct rays of sunlight. It withstands temperature differences from sub-zero to 165°F. It will yellow, however, after two to three weeks of exposure to direct sunlight. The mechanical properties of Styrofoam vary with its density — the higher the density, the greater the strength.

The artist will find that Styrofoam is easily cut or textured with an ordinary knife, saw, sandpaper, or soldering gun. Many sculptors have made their own hot-wire cutters and special tips for electric soldering guns, designed especially to cut this material. A photo of an electric hot-wire cutter in operation is shown in Chapter 18.

Commercially designed hot-wire cutters are available from the Dura-

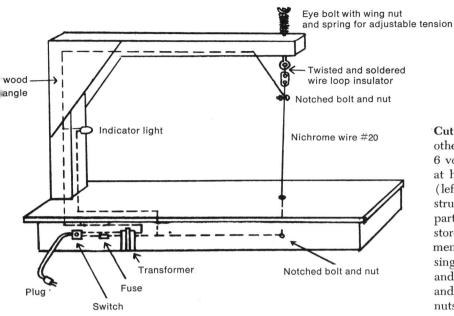

Eye bolt with wing nut
and spring for adjustable tension

wood
angle

Twisted and soldered
wire loop insulator

Notched bolt and nut

Indicator light

Nichrome wire #20

Transformer

Notched bolt and nut

Plug

Fuse

Switch

**Cutting intricate forms from Styrofoam** and other cellular plastic foams is easy with this 6 volt hot wire cutter, which you can make at home if you are handy. As the diagram (left) indicates, you can make the entire structure out of wood, plus the following parts, available from your local radio parts store and hardware store: transformer, filament 6.3V @ 10 amps; switch, double pole, single throw; red indicator light; fuse holder and fuse; insulator; nickel chrome wire; plug and rubber coated wire; notched bolts and nuts; spring.

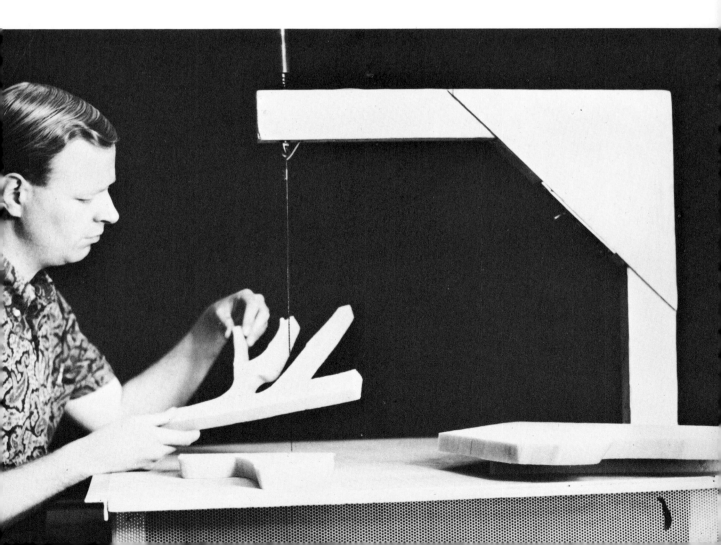

Tech Corporation, 1555 N.W. First Avenue, Boca Raton, Florida. Plans for making your own cutters may be obtained by writing directly to the Dow Chemical Company, Plastics Department, Midland, Michigan. It should be noted that proper allowances should be made for ventilation when using these cutters, since fumes from burning Styrofoam are considered toxic.

Aside from using mechanical or hot-wire tools for texturing this cellular plastic, the sculptor can produce interesting surface variations chemically. Lacquer thinner, turpentine, and acetone dissolve Styrofoam; the controlled use of these chemicals may produce interesting surface textures of a lacy, cobweb-like nature. Standard sizes of Styrofoam slabs and blocks come in 1″ to 4″ thicknesses, 1½′ to 2′ widths, and lengths up to 9′.

**Coatings and Adhesives for Styrofoam**

Styrofoam surfaces are attacked by many solvents within paints, and care should be taken to select a proper paint coating. Best results are obtained by using water emulsion paints such as vinyl, latex, or acrylic. Epoxy resin pastes and plastic-modified concrete stucco may also be used as a surface putty.

It is wise to experiment on scrap Styrofoam first to determine whether the paint or surface coating will bond properly, without adversely affecting the cellular plastic. Sections of Styrofoam may be bonded together with epoxy adhesives, acrylic or polyvinyl acetate pastes, or internal setting asphalt adhesives, such as Borden's Insulgrip.

**Expanded Polystyrene as a Burn-out Material**

Many sculptors and jewelers are using expanded polystyrene as a temporary material to create three-dimensional designs which are later cast in metal. An investment mold, generally made of a mixture of plaster of Paris, asbestos, and powdered fire clay, thus capable of withstanding the temperatures of the molten metal, is cast over the Styrofoam construction. Molten bronze, aluminum, or other metal is poured into the mold; the Styrofoam burns away and is replaced by the molten metal, which becomes the final work. The entire process is best done in a professional foundry.

**Rigid Urethane Foams**

These newer cellular plastics are formed by the reaction of isocyanates with hydroxyl bearing compounds such as polyesters. Millions of tiny, closed cells, filled with harmless gas, are produced to create these cellular plastics. The cell sizes of the urethanes may be controlled during the manufacturing process to create a great variety of densities. Typical urethane insulation slabs have an average density of about two pounds per cubic foot, although they may be tailor made to densities up to 32 pounds per cubic foot.

A distinct advantage of using rigid urethanes for sculpture is that this material is not corroded by many chemicals — as is the expanded polystyrene — and subsequently, polyester coatings, lacquers, sealers, and other such coatings may be used. Urethanes are lightweight materials, non-toxic, and widely used for thermal insulation.

Ordinary hand or power tools may be used to work the materials, and the lower density slabs are easily cut with hacksaw blades, electric kitchen knives, or similar household implements. If you use power tools, high speed equipment is best for obtaining smoother cuts. Standard band saw equipment, with blade speeds from 2000′ to 5000′ per minute, is generally used by commercial fabricators. Various grades of sandpaper — and even blocks of the foam itself — can be used to sand urethane surfaces. Note, however, that hot-wire cutters, soldering guns, and other such tools *should not* be used with rigid urethane; the fumes are extremely toxic. Mechanical tools are best suited for working this material; electric carving knives are excellent devices for cutting larger slabs.

Recommended adhesives for rigid urethanes include epoxy, urea, resorcinol or phenolic base resin adhesives, contact rubber glues, and asphalt emulsion adhesives.

Standard slabs of commercially available rigid urethane vary from ¾″ to 6″ in thickness, and up to 3′ x 6′.

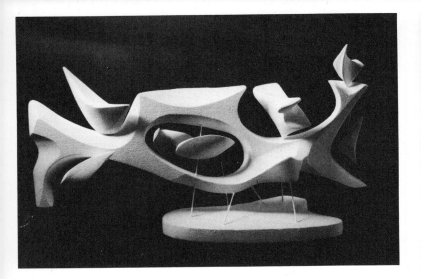

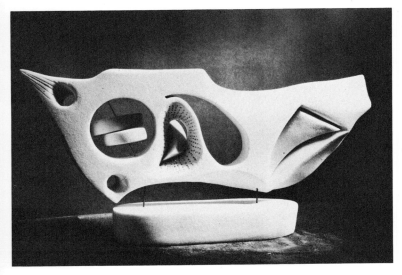

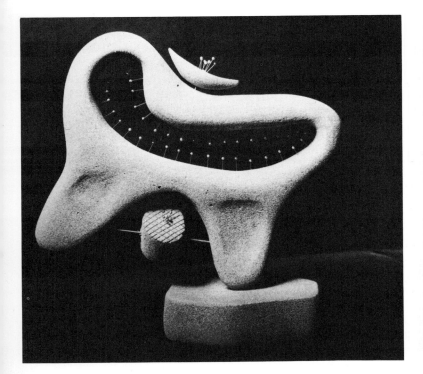

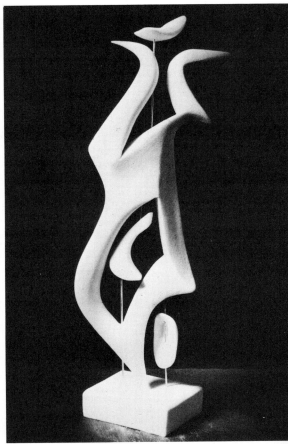

**Sculpture** (left) in rigid polyurethane, student work from the synthetic media workshop, University of Calgary, Alberta.

**Sculpture** (right) by Eugenio Degani, bronze. Degani originally created the sculpture in polystyrene. It was cast in bronze by a burn-out process whereby the cellular plastic is encased in a mold and volatized as the molten metal is poured in. The mold was made of asbestos, clay, and plaster of Paris.

**La Timone** (below) work in process by Gerard Singer. The artist is shown standing in front of the mold made of polystyrene. Singer has developed a process in which the mold is made first, then coated with a heavy putty of epoxy resin. When the epoxy has polymerized, the Styrofoam is dissolved with acetone to reveal the final sculptural form.

**Wind Gate** (left) by Roger Bolomey, 8'7" x 7'2", polyurethane and aluminum, courtesy Royal S. Marks Gallery, New York. Constructed in three sections, the sculpture is made of poured polyurethane, shaped and textured.

**Architectural Wall** (below) by William Mitchell, 18' x 6', concrete cast in polyurethane mold, Harlow New Town project, London. The concrete surface was hammered for textural effect.

**Triad** (right) by Vytautas Jonynas, architectural sculpture for Vatican Pavilion, New York World's Fair, 1965, 21' x 27', polystyrene covered with epoxy resin. Molded first in polystyrene, this work was later covered with catalyzed epoxy resin, and given additional textural interest by pressing slab glass and mosaic tessarae into the wet surface. If executed in stone, the work would have weighed 18 to 20 tons. In plastic resins, it totaled only 3000 pounds and required only toggle bolts for installation to the wall of the pavilion.

# 18 Casting an Architectural Wall from a Cellular Plastic Mold

Albert Vrana of Coconut Grove, Florida, has used expanded polystyrene as a mold material to cast a concrete relief for the Federal Office Building at Jacksonville, Florida. He describes his method. . . .

The architectural requirement was to design and create a relief wall with a non-repetitive design, measuring 16' x 550', for a federal office building. The theme was to be *The Evolution of Government,* portraying the development of society. Implicit in the work, therefore, was the idea of the formation of civilization, the primal need of human beings to co-exist ultimately as nations, wherein their resources and talents would be shared and developed, and their lives protected through federation.

In creating this bas relief, I tried to symbolize the struggles and forces which have been significant in the creation of a democratic system of government. Symbolism is prevalent throughout the work, and the spectator who enters the office building and sees the work will identify with the life-size figures in the foreground of the panel. These figures represent the citizens, witnesses under whose watchful eyes the forces of history revolve. Design symbols of creative forces, destructive forces, and the metamorphosis of our civilization are integrated into the work.

**The Mold Material**

A word regarding the material. Because of the large scale requirements of the project, the mold was made of polystyrene, a lightweight cellular plastic. The final work was cast in concrete, heightened with textures of exposed aggregate. Casting concrete into polystyrene molds is now becoming standard practice with many architectural sculptors, and the processes are fairly easy to perform.

One of the most significant factors in the use of polystyrene as mold material is low cost. It is an inexpensive material — in some cases, even less costly than a rigid mold for repetitive castings. Because of the material's light weight, it would be quite possible — just from the dollars and cents point of view — for me to design and make the molds here in my studio in South Florida, and then to ship them anywhere in the world for final casting and assembly.

**Planning the Design**

I began by making rough sketches of design possibilities for the architectural wall. I eventually made a small scale model, showing the relationship of the wall to the office building. Direct work on the project began with scale drawings, drawn to a proportion of 1″ to 1′. Since there were to be 27 sections of the wall, 27 drawings were made. The drawings were then covered with a grid of 3″ squares. Polystyrene sheets were gridded off in 3″ squares; thus a 1″ to 1′ scale was established for enlargement and transfer of the scale drawings. This ancient grid system of enlargement worked well in transferring my sketches to the cellular plastic material. The original polystyrene sheets were 1″ thick.

**Making the Molds**

Additional 1″ slabs of polystyrene were cut to predetermined shapes and glued onto the surface of the first plastic sheets that carried the drawings, now making the plastic 2″ thick at various points, or even thicker. A color code system was devised to indicate to assistants the depth to be carved on the relief panels. An electronic solder gun was equipped with a special tip by brazing the blade of a stainless steel kitchen knife to the heating element of a heavy duty soldering gun. This was used to cut the material. Portable electric drills, equipped with large carborundum grinding and sanding discs, were used to carve and shape the surface of the polystyrene.

Once the mold was completed, some areas were painted with a special coating developed by the artist, a concrete retarder with a sugar base. This allowed the subsequent casting in concrete to expose the rock aggregate at those "painted" areas where the concrete would not adhere. Emulsified petroleum oil, available at building supply houses, was brushed over the surface of the polystyrene mold to act as a release agent, preventing the plastic mold from bonding to the concrete casting.

**Casting Concrete**

The 27 finished molds were moved from the studio to a concrete yard, where the concrete casting took place. Trained workmen used truck-mixed concrete aggregate and carefully poured it into the molds under my supervision.

After a preliminary pouring of 4″, reinforcing rods were placed in the mixture and additional concrete was poured, reaching an ultimate thickness of 6″. The concrete mixture was of the following proportions: one part cement, one part sand, and two parts rock aggregate. The panels were allowed to cure at the yard for about 10 days and then were transported by truck to the building site for installation.

The purpose of these architectural panels was twofold: they became an actual wall, and they were ornamental. The panels were secured to reinforced concrete beams by welding clips (pieces of angle iron about 10″ long). They were then cleaned with muriatic acid and water, allowed to dry, and finally painted with a solution of 5% silicone to impregnate the porous concrete and yield a richer surface.

**Step 1:** Albert Vrana makes scale drawings, drawn to a proportion of 1″ to 1′, for an architectural wall for the Federal Office Building in Jacksonville, Florida. The final work measures 16′ x 550′ and is cast of concrete from a mold of polystyrene. A scale model was also constructed to visualize the work.

**Step 2:** Scale drawings gridded in 3″ squares, corresponding to 3′ squares on the plastic sheets have been transferred to the polystyrene. The transfer was made by freehand sketching, with careful reference to the original scale drawing. Polystyrene shapes are cut from additional sheets of cellular plastic and will be laminated to the design to build up greater thickness. Later, these will be sanded to produce smooth contours.

**Step 3:** Electric soldering guns are equipped with specially designed steel tips for cutting the polystyrene sheets. Other tools include electric drills with carborundum grinding and sanding discs.

**Step 4:** (above) The panels are ready for casting. Dark areas are specially painted with concrete retarder to aid in exposing the rock aggregate texture in the final casting.

**Step 5:** (left) After a thickness of 4″ of concrete has been poured, reinforcement rod is laid over the mixture and additional concrete is poured. The final thickness of the panel is 6″. Twenty-seven separate molds are poured at the cement yard.

**Step 6:** (left) Vrana strips the polystyrene sheets from the cast panels. After curing for 10 days, the panels are transported by truck to the building site for final installation.

**Evolution of Government Panel** (below) Here is one of the 27 panels. Notice the detail of the exposed rock aggregate.

**Step 7:** (right) Vrana's completed panel is hoisted into final position by a crane. The architectural wall contrasts effectively with the building.

**Step 8:** (left) Serving as an actual wall, as well as an architectural embellishment, the panels are secured to the building with welding angle clips. A solution of muriatic acid is used to clean the surface of the concrete panels.

**Evolution of Government** (below) by Albert Vrana, architectural wall at the Federal Office Building, Jacksonville, Florida, 16' x 550', concrete cast in polystyrene. (See plate in color section.)

# Dyes, Pigments, and Coatings 19

By using colorants containing pigments or dyes, the artist may give his work in plastics a full range of color. Colorants which contain pigments vary in several ways from those which contain dyes. Pigments are finely ground colors which are insoluble in the coating material and generally produce opaque effects. Dyes, on the other hand, dissolve within the resin, creating transparent or translucent effects.

Two basic methods of coloring plastic are: adding integral color within the plastic; and applying surface coatings.

**Integral Color within Plastic**

Both pigments and dyes may be added to the liquid resins — before catalyzing — to obtain transparent, translucent, or opaque colors. Most shops that handle plastic resins also carry a line of colorants in dry, paste, or liquid form; these colorants are especially designed for liquid resins such as polyester, epoxy, or acrylic monomer. Here are the desirable characteristics of such colorants:

(1) They are compatible to resin systems.
(2) They withstand the heat of polymerization.
(3) They are light-fast.
(4) They withstand the effects of chemicals such as peroxide catalysts.
(5) They do not affect the curing properties of the resin.
(6) They disperse easily within the resin.
(7) They are economical and readily available.

Colorants for use with liquid plastics are listed in Sources of Supplies.

Generally speaking, paste colorants are much easier to handle than dry colors. Pastes which are especially made for use with liquid plastics are ground and dispersed in a plastic resin base, and are easily dispersed within resins such as polyester, epoxy, or methyl methacrylate monomer.

**Adverse Effects of Colorants**

Many pigments have adverse effects on liquid plastics and should not be used. Some either inhibit or accelerate the curing cycle, while others are not stable within the resin, or may be adversely affected by the strong chemicals within the resin itself. Phthalocyanine greens, for example, inhibit the curing cycle of polyester, and as little as 0.02 per cent of this pigment may prevent complete polymerization of the resin.

Before using pigments as colorants for plastic, it is always wise to test first. However, commercially available paste-color concentrates and dispersed dyes are prepared to withstand adverse effects of chemicals within the plastic, and prepared for use with various plastics.

**Dyes for Liquid Resins**

Dyes should dissolve completely in compatible resins, producing transparent or translucent effects. Dyes such as the Perox Dyes are highly recommended because of their excellent color, high temperature resistance, and resistance to peroxide chemicals. The charts on the following pages are a general guide for the use of pigments and dyes in plastics, prepared by James E. Simpson of the Ferro Corporation.

**Surface Coatings for Rigid Plastics**

As the basic characteristics of plastic resins vary, requirements for surface coatings will also differ. Listed below are some of the commonly used plastics and suggested surface coatings.

*Polyester and Epoxy:*

(1) Dry colors, pastes, or dyes dispersed in catalyzed polyester resins.
(2) Dry colors, pastes, or dyes dispersed in catalyzed epoxy resins.
(3) Commercially available paints containing plastic bases.
(4) Epoxy based paints requiring hardener.
(5) Water emulsified paints such as vinyl, acetate, or acrylic copolymer.

*Solid Acrylic:*

(1) Dry color, dyes, or pastes dispersed in catalyzed polyester or methyl methacrylate monomer.
(2) Commercially available plastic sign paint (see Grip-Flex in "Sources of Supplies").

*Rigid Foamed Plastic — Polystyrene:*

(1) Water emulsified paints such as latex, polyvinyl acetate, acrylic copolymers, and acrylic gesso or paste extender.
(2) Epoxy and epoxy filled mixtures.
(3) Modified Portland cement stuccos.

*Rigid Foamed Plastic — Polyurethane:*

(1) Coatings listed above for polystyrene.
(2) Polyester and polyester filled mixtures.

*Paste Coatings for Plastics:* Heavy viscosity surface coatings include:

(1) Acrylic paste extender.
(2) Filled polyester resin (resinated metal, etc.).
(3) Filled epoxy resin mixtures (resinated metal, etc.).
(4) Syntactic foams.
(5) Latex-modified Portland cement (for expanded plastics).

# RECOMMENDED USES FOR ORGANIC PIGMENTS

| | | THERMOPLASTICS | | | | | | | | | | | | THERMOSETS | | | | | | |
|---|---|---|---|---|---|---|---|---|---|---|---|---|---|---|---|---|---|---|---|---|
| | | ACETAL [a] | ACRYLICS | CELLULOSICS | NYLONS | POLYETHYLENE Low Density | POLYETHYLENE High Density | POLYPROPYLENE | POLYCARBONATE | FLUOROCARBONS | POLYSTYRENE General Purpose | POLYSTYRENE Impact Resistant | VINYLS Flexible | VINYLS Rigid | AMINO RESINS | DIALLYL PHTHALATE | PHENOL-FORMALDEHYDE | POLYESTER-ALKYD | SILICONE MOLDING COMPOUNDS | EPOXY | POLYURETHANE (elastomers and foams) |
| Black | BONE BLACK | | | | | | | | NR | NR | | | | | | | | NR | NR | | |
| | CARBON BLACK | | | | | | | | | NR | | | | | | | | NR | NR | | |
| Blue, Green | INDANTHRONE blue | | | | NR | | | | NR | NR | | | | | | | | | | | |
| | PIGMENT GREEN B dark green | | | NR | NR | NR | NR | NR | NR | NR | | | NR | NR | | | | | | | |
| | PTA/PMA TONERS blue, green | | NR | NR | NR | NR | NR | NR | NR | NR | NR | NR | NR | NR | | | | NR | NR | | |
| | PHTHALOCYANINE green | | | | | | | | | | | | | | | | | | | | |
| | PHTHALOCYANINE blue | | | | | | | | | NR | | | | | | | | | | | |
| Orange, Yellow | NICKEL-AZO green yellow | | | | | NR | NR | NR | NR | NR | | | | | | | | | | | |
| | HANSA YELLOW light yellow | | | | NR | NR | NR | NR | NR | NR | | NR | NR | NR | | | | NR | NR | | |
| | BENZIDINE YELLOW, XYLIDIDE, deep-light yellow | NR | NR | NR | NR | NR | NR | NR | NR | | | | NR | NR | | | | | | | |
| | BENZIDINE YELLOW light yellow | | | NR | NR | NR | NR | NR | NR | NR | | | NR | NR | | | | | | | |
| Violets, Maroons, Reds | NAPHTHOL dark - light red | | | | NR | | | NR | NR | NR | NR | | | NR | | | | | | | |
| | PYRAZOLONE light red | | | | NR | | | NR | NR | NR | NR | | | NR | | | | | | | |
| | RED LAKE C light red | | | | NR | | | NR | NR | NR | NR | | NR | NR | | | | | | | |
| | PTMA TONERS violet - medium red | | NR | | NR | NR | NR | NR | NR | NR | NR | NR | NR | NR | | | | | | | |
| | TOLUIDINE maroon - light red | NR | NR | NR | NR | NR | NR | NR | NR | NR | NR | NR | NR | NR | | | | | NR | | |
| | THIOINDIGOID copper - maroon | | | NR | | | | | NR | NR | | | | NR | | | | | | | |
| | HELIO BORDEAUX maroon | | | NR | | | | | NR | NR | | | | NR | | | | | | | |
| | ALIZARINE MAROON maroon | | | NR | | | NR | NR | NR | NR | NR | NR | | | | | | | | | |
| | MADDER LAKE red | | | NR | NR | NR | NR | NR | NR | NR | NR | NR | NR | NR | | | | | | | |
| | PIGMENT SCARLET bluish red | | | NR | | | NR | NR | NR | NR | | | | NR | | | | | | | |
| | Na, Ba, Ca LITHOLS maroon - light red | | NR | NR | | NR | NR | NR | NR | NR | | NR | NR | NR | | | | | | | |
| | LITHOL RUBINE bluish red | | | NR | | | NR | NR | NR | NR | | | | NR | | | | | | | |
| | B.O.N. (2B-Mn Salt) maroon - light red | NR | | NR | NR | NR | NR | NR | NR | NR | | | | NR | | | NR | | | | |
| | B.O.N. (2B-Ca Salt) maroon - light red | NR | | NR | | | | NR | NR | NR | | | NR | | | | NR | | | | |
| | CHLORINATED PARA light red | NR | NR | NR | NR | NR | NR | NR | NR | NR | NR | NR | NR | NR | | | | | | | |
| | PARA RED light red | NR | NR | NR | NR | NR | NR | NR | NR | NR | NR | NR | NR | NR | | | | | NR | | |
| | QUINACRIDONE maroon - medium red | NR | | NR | | NR | NR | NR | NR | | | | | | | | | | | | |

## RECOMMENDED USES FOR INORGANIC PIGMENTS

| | | ACETAL [a] | ACRYLICS | CELLULOSICS | NYLONS | POLYETHYLENE Low Density | POLYETHYLENE High Density | POLYPROPYLENE | POLYCARBONATE | FLUOROCARBONS | POLYSTYRENE General Purpose | POLYSTYRENE Impact Resistant | VINYLS Flexible | VINYLS Rigid | AMINO RESINS | DIALLYL PHTHALATE | PHENOL-FORMALDEHYDE | POLYESTER-ALKYD | SILICONE MOLDING COMPOUNDS | EPOXY | POLYURETHANE (elastomers and foams) |
|---|---|---|---|---|---|---|---|---|---|---|---|---|---|---|---|---|---|---|---|---|---|
| Black | IRON OXIDE | NR | | | | | | | | | | | | | | | | | | | |
| | CERAMIC BLACK | NR | NR | | | | | | | | | | | | | | | | | | |
| Blue, Green | HYDRATED CHROME OXIDE green | | | | NR | NR | | NR | | | | | NR | NR | | | | | | | |
| | CHROME GREEN green | | NR | NR | NR | NR | NR | NR | NR | NR | | | | NR | | | | | | | |
| | CHROMIUM OXIDE dull green | | | | | | | | | | | | | | | | | | | | |
| | ULTRAMARINE BLUE blue | | | | | | | | | | | | | | | | | | | | |
| | IRON BLUE blue | | | NR | NR | | | NR | NR | NR | | | | | | | | | | | |
| | CHROME-COBALT-ALUMINA turquoise | | | | | | | | | | | | | | | | | | | | |
| | COBALT ALUMINATE blue | | | | | | | | | | | | | | | | | | | | |

151

## RECOMMENDED USES FOR INORGANIC PIGMENTS (cont.)

| | | ACETAL [a] | ACRYLICS | CELLULOSICS | NYLONS | POLYETHYLENE Low Density | POLYETHYLENE High Density | POLYPROPYLENE | POLYCARBONATE | FLUOROCARBONS | POLYSTYRENE General Purpose | POLYSTYRENE Impact Resistant | VINYLS Flexible | VINYLS Rigid | AMINO RESINS | DIALLYL PHTHALATE | PHENOL-FORMALDEHYDE | POLYESTER-ALKYD | SILICONE MOLDING COMPOUNDS | EPOXY | POLYURETHANE (elastomers and foams) |
|---|---|---|---|---|---|---|---|---|---|---|---|---|---|---|---|---|---|---|---|---|---|
| Brown | NATURAL INORGANICS – SIENNAS, iron oxides, umbers | | | | NR | | | | NR | NR | | NR | | | | | | | | NR | |
| Brown | NATURAL INORGANICS – OCHRES – buff, brown | | NR | NR | NR | NR | NR | | NR | NR | | NR | | | | | | | | NR | |
| Brown | IRON OXIDE buff, brown | | | | | | | | | | | | | | | | | | | | |
| Orange, Yellow, Buff | CERAMIC YELLOWS (antimony titanium–chrome oxide) | | | | | | | | | | | | | | | | | | | | |
| Orange, Yellow, Buff | TITANIUM PIGMENTS yellow, buff | | | | | | | | | | | | | | | | | | | | |
| Orange, Yellow, Buff | ZINC CHROMATE yellow | | | | NR | | NR | NR | NR | | NR | | NR | NR | | | | | | | |
| Orange, Yellow, Buff | MOLYBDATE orange | | NR | NR | NR | | | | | | | NR | | | | | | | | NR | |
| Orange, Yellow, Buff | CHROME orange, yellow | | NR | NR | NR | | | | | | | NR | | | | | | | | NR | |
| Orange, Yellow, Buff | CADMIUM SULFIDE yellow | | | | | | | | | | | | | | | | | | | | |
| Red, Red Orange | MANGANESE violet | | | | | | | | | | | | | | | | | | | | |
| Red, Red Orange | CHROME–TIN pink | | | | | | | | | | | | | | | | | | | | |
| Red, Red Orange | CADMIUM MERCURY maroon, red, orange | | | | | | | | | | | | | | | | | | | | |
| Red, Red Orange | CADMIUM SULFO–SELENIDE maroon, red, orange | | | | | | | | | | | | | | | | | | | | |
| White | ZINC OXIDE | | NR | NR | | NR | NR | NR | NR | NR | NR | NR | NR | NR | NR | NR | NR | NR | NR | NR | NR |
| White | ZINC SULFIDE | | NR | NR | | NR | NR | | NR | NR | NR | NR | NR | NR | NR | NR | | NR | NR | NR | |
| White | TITANIUM DIOXIDE | | | | | | | | | | | | | | | | | | | | |

## RECOMMENDED USES FOR DYES (Soluble)

| | ACETAL [a] | ACRYLICS | CELLULOSICS | NYLONS | POLYETHYLENE Low Density | POLYETHYLENE High Density | POLYPROPYLENE | POLYCARBONATE | FLUOROCARBONS | POLYSTYRENE General Purpose | POLYSTYRENE Impact Resistant | VINYLS Flexible | VINYLS Rigid | AMINO RESINS | DIALLYL PHTHALATE | PHENOL-FORMALDEHYDE | POLYESTER-ALKYD | SILICONE MOLDING COMPOUNDS | EPOXY | POLYURETHANE |
|---|---|---|---|---|---|---|---|---|---|---|---|---|---|---|---|---|---|---|---|---|
| NIGROSINES AND INDULINES wide color range | NR | b | | NR | NR | NR | NR | NR | NR | NR | NR | | | | NR | | NR | NR | NR | |
| BASIC DYE BASES wide color range | NR | | | NR | NR | NR | NR | NR | NR | | NR | NR | | | | NR | | NR | NR | |
| BASIC DYES wide color range | NR | NR | | NR | NR | NR | NR | NR | NR | NR | NR | | | | NR | NR | NR | NR | NR | |
| ACID, CHROME AND DIRECT wide color range | NR | NR | NR | | NR | NR | NR | NR | NR | NR | NR | | | | NR | NR | NR | NR | NR | |
| ACETATE wide color range | NR | | | NR | NR | NR | NR | NR | | NR | NR | | | | | NR | | NR | | |
| ANTHRAQUINONE, green, yellow-red, blue, brown | NR | | | NR | NR | NR | NR | NR | | | NR | | | NR | | NR | | NR | | |
| AZO, brown, yellow-red, green, blue | NR | | | | NR | NR | NR | NR | NR | | NR | NR | | NR | | NR | | NR | | |

**KEY:**

■ Colorant family is widely used to color resin indicated.

□ Colorant has limited use in resin indicated. Before it is used, the performance and resistance characteristics of the colorant should be checked in specific application.

NR  Colorant family is not recommended for use in resin indicated.

**NOTES:**

a  Colorants for acetal resins -- individual colorants must be tested before using in the acetal resins because of variations in amount and type of impurities contained in the colorant from one colorant supplier to another.

b  Nigrosine and induline dyes are not recommended for use in cellulose propionate.

# Molds and Releases 20

The essential task of a mold is to make the transfer of a sculptural form from one material to another. For example, the artist may begin his work with clay, which is easily modeled; later, the form may be cast into its permanent state by using another material such as polyester resin. In this instance, clay serves only a temporary function; its inherent character as an art medium is not of permanent importance to the artist. Although he works with one material, he thinks in terms of another, and develops a sculptural form which will bring out the inherent qualities of the ultimate medium.

Molds may be classified into two basic groups: rigid and flexible. They may be further classified as permanent or temporary molds. Waste molds are temporary. These are used only once and are destroyed in the process of removing the cast sculpture. Section molds or piece molds (and most flexible molds) are considered permanent because more than one casting may be taken from them. Mold materials which are generally suitable for casting with plastics are described in the text to follow. Sources of materials are listed in the back of the book in the section entitled, "Sources of Supplies."

**Rigid Molds**

Rigid molds for casting plastic resins are generally made of the following materials: (1) plaster of Paris; (2) plastic; (3) metal; (4) clay; (5) glass.

The most commonly used material is plaster of Paris. It is inexpensive, easy to use, and readily available from building supply houses. Plaster of Paris may be used to make both waste molds and section molds. For making *waste molds,* Red Top casting plaster is recommended. The material sets quickly (about 15 minutes) and produces a rigid mold which is fairly soft, facilitating its removal by chipping. For piece molds, a harder plaster such as Hydrocal or Ultracal (products of the U.S. Gypsum Company) are recommended.

In designing piece molds, take care to avoid undercuts, which would lock castings within the mold. To insure proper registration of the various sections of the piece mold, some registration device should be incorporated in the mold design. Positive and negative register plugs (like the notches described in Chapter 6) are typical means of solving this problem. Plaster molds should always be allowed to dry thoroughly before they are treated with parting agents and used for casting with plastic resins.

Permanent, lightweight molds may be made from polyester fibreglass. Depending on the size of the sculpture, lamination (varying from three to ten layers of fibreglass cloth) may be used. If laminated fibreglass is used on plaster of Paris, mold sealer and mold release should be used on the plaster to effect release. As polyester fibreglass molds cannot be made directly on damp clay sculptures, the artist must make an "in between" mold and plaster casting; the original clay sculpture is transferred from clay to plaster by means of a plaster waste mold. Laminations of polyester fibreglass are made over this to create the final lightweight plastic mold. Polyester fibreglass molds may be made directly on other rigid materials, including polyurethane cellular plastic. Over polyurethane, a hot mixture of wax (beeswax and paraffin, mixed 1:1) should be applied as a release agent.

Semi-rigid molds may be made by vacuum forming thermoplastic sheets and using them for casting plastic resins. Kitchen utensils, such as glass trays, bowls, etc., may also be employed as molds. These should be lightly waxed before using. As most of the casting resins contract slightly upon polymerization, release from negative forms is relatively easy.

**Mold Releases**

Mold releases, commonly called parting agents, are grouped in four basic categories:

(1) *Films:* These may be either flexible or rigid, consisting of materials such as cellophane, vinyl, or tinfoil.

(2) *Film forming liquids:* These liquids are brushed or sprayed over sealed molds. Chemicals which are commonly used are polyvinyl alcohol (PVA) and cellulose acetate.

(3) *Powders:* Zinc stearate is most often used.

(4) *Greasy lubricants:* Petroleum jelly, silicone grease, waxes such as carnauba, candellilla, and damar.

Porous molds should be sealed first before mold releases are applied. Clear lacquer, cut 1:1 with lacquer thinner, makes an effective sealer. Two or three coats should be applied to plaster molds. Before use, a mold release should be checked to see that it withstands the chemical and heat attack of the plastic resin to be used.

**Parting Agents for Plaster Molds**

As mentioned before, plaster molds should be bone dry and properly sealed before any parting agents are used. An effective method of preparing a plaster mold for casting with plastic resin is as follows:

(1) The plaster mold is allowed to dry and given three coats of clear lacquer to seal porosity.

(2) Two coats of paste wax are applied, and the mold surface is then polished. A wax with a high melting temperature is recommended.

(3) Two coats of polyvinyl alcohol (PVA) are brushed or sprayed evenly over the surface.

The plaster mold is now ready for casting. If a section mold (or piece) has been made, PVA mold release should be applied each time the mold is used.

Many excellent commercial mold releases are available which dispense with the multiple steps outlined above. Two sources for such materials are: Specialty Products Company, 15 Exchange Place, Jersey City, New Jersey, and Dow Chemical Products Division, Midland, Michigan.

**Flexible Molds**

Typical flexible molds for casting with plastic resins may be made from (1) silicone rubber, (2) vinyl chloride, and (3) polyurethane rubber compounds.

Unless the work is small, most flexible molds require a supporting mold of plaster of Paris. This mold (or "plaster jacket") keeps the flexible mold from losing its shape under the weight and pressure of the cast material.

Styrene in polyester resins has a corrosive effect on some flexible mold materials; it pays to experiment with small amounts of material before embarking on large scale projects.

**Silicone Rubber Molds**

The Dow Chemical Company of Midland, Michigan, manufactures a silicone rubber mold material called Silastic RTV. This is a fluid, fast setting, vulcanizing silicone rubber which cures at room temperature. A catalyst is added to Silastic RTV, and vulcanization is effected within 24 hours.

Such rubber molds may be made from plaster, wood, wax, soap, metal, glass, or plastic. Although no parting agent is normally required for making molds from most of these materials, releases should be used on sculptures with an especially intricate structure. An effective release may be made by mixing three to five parts of household detergent in 100 parts of water. This is then brushed onto the surface of the sculpture to be cast. The sculpture is placed in a container and Silastic RTV is applied by pouring until the container is full.

The chief disadvantage of this material is cost. Unless the work is small, Silastic RTV is a fairly expensive material to use.

**Vinyl Chloride Molds**

Vinyl chloride, a flexible mold making material, is of the hot-melt type. Shreds of vinyl chloride are melted at a temperature of 350°F. to create a hot liquid which is then poured over plaster or other materials capable of withstanding temperatures of 400°F. As in the preceding example, the sculpture is placed in a box (or other suitable container) into which the hot liquid is poured.

General Fabricators, Inc., of Van Nuys, California, manufactures a reusable vinyl chloride mold making material called Plastiflex, available in several formulations. The shredded chunks of this material are melted in a double boiler, an electric roaster, or an electric oven at temperatures between

**Architectural Wall** (left) by William Mitchell for Hapstead Swim Bath, Hapstead, England, 200' x 14' x 3', concrete against polyester fibreglass molds. The tops of the relief slabs form seats on a terrace. Basil Spence, architect.

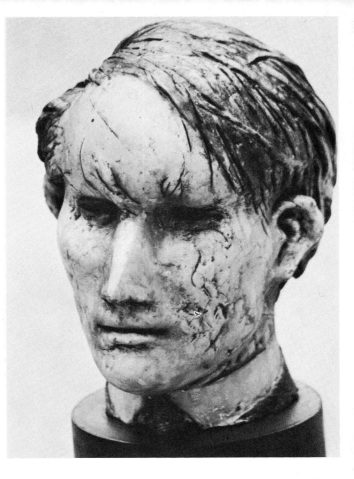

**The Critic** by Frank Gallo, life size, epoxy, Los Angeles County Museum, photo courtesy Graham Gallery, New York. Epoxy and polyester will faithfully reproduce the character of a clay original from an accurate mold.

**Mario Cazzani** by Anthony Gray, life size, resinated bronze. Polyester and bronze powder, cast from a plaster mold.

340°F. and 360°F. Equipment for melting the vinyl chloride should include an immersion thermometer, which is used to check the temperature.

Although the material is reclaimable and may be used many times, overheating will ruin it. If a double boiler is used, an oil bath, rather than water, should be used to transfer heat to the vinyl chloride. Castor oil (or high flash-point petroleum oil) is recommended by the manufacturer. The oil temperature should be carefully checked and not allowed to rise above 400°F.

A much easier method of melting vinyl chloride is to put the material in an open container which is then placed in an electric oven or roaster. No double boiler is required. Temperature controls should be set at 350°F. and the mixture should be stirred continuously. Additional chunks of the shredded vinyl chloride are added and stirred into the mixture until the proper volume is reached. It is necessary to make a sufficient quantity of the hot mixture to make one continuous, uninterrupted pouring.

Before applying this mold material, plaster sculpture should be treated with linseed oil soap, which is wiped on and then polished. High gloss surfaces are produced by first impregnating the plaster with Cal Resin Glaze, series 200. This plaster impregnating resin is available from the Cal Resin Company, 4543 Brazil Street, Los Angeles, California. Models should be pre-heated to about 200°F. before the hot, melted vinyl chloride is poured.

**Polyurethane Rubber Mold Materials**

Several new flexible mold making materials are being formulated of a polyurethane rubber base. These are available in a liquid, two-component system, and are excellent for casting with polyester or epoxy resins.

The Smooth-On Manufacturing Company, 572 Communipaw Avenue, Jersey City, New Jersey, manufactures Smooth-On PMC 703, which may be used over models of plaster, wood, metal, or plastic. After mixing the two-component system, curing occurs within 16 hours at normal room temperature. Pot life is about one half hour at 77°F. As a parting agent, petroleum jelly or silicone grease is recommended over non-porous materials such as metals, glass, plastics, etc. Plaster, wood, and other porous surfaces should be sealed first with potter's soap or lacquer before the parting agent is applied.

The Devcon Corporation of Danvers, Massachusetts, manufactures a urethane mold material called Flexane. This material is used with a catalyst and will cure to a rubbery solid overnight, at normal room temperature. Flexane products are available in liquids for pouring, and in putties for troweling.

Some artists are experimenting with U. S. Rubber Company's Ultrathene EVA, an ultrathene-wax formulation which may be brushed directly onto clay sculptures.

Natural rubber latex is not normally used to make flexible molds for casting with plastic resins because the chemicals within the resins have a corrosive action on the latex. It may be used, however, when suitable release agents are employed.

# Molding Pellets, Sprayable Vinyl, Vacuum Forming, and "Op" 21

Obviously, many methods and materials have not been included. Unfortunately, there is not enough space in one volume to cover all the possibilities of the vast plastics field. Therefore, the text omits detailed descriptions of several areas of plastics technology which may have implications for the fine arts. Among these are the uses of molding pellets, uses of sprayable vinyl plastic, vacuum forming techniques, and the uses of multi-lensed or moiré patterned plastic sheets. There are, of course, many others, and an insight into these possibilities may be gained by reading some of the books listed in the bibliography.

Rather than ignore some of these areas completely, I would like to take a parting shot at the four areas mentioned above.

**Working with Plastic Molding Pellets**

Among the many plastic pellets, beads, and powders manufactured by the plastics industry for injection molding or extrusion, there are several that may be used in the artist's studio.

Polystyrene pellets are among those most easily fused in the home oven. These pellets are approximately ⅛" in diameter and about ³⁄₁₆" long. They are available in a variety of colors and are readily fused at temperatures between 250°F. and 400°F.

A typical method of using these pellets is to place them in a pan or on metallic foil within a frame and heat them in an oven until the pellets partially melt and fuse together. By varying the time they are left in the oven, a variey of effects may be achieved.

Polystyrene pellets, polyethylene, and other plastic pellets are available from Shell Chemical Company, as well as from several other manufacturers. These materials are ordinarily available from the manufacturer only in large orders; however, artists interested in this material should seek *local* jobbers or distributors.

**Sprayable Vinyl**

The sculptor, Piotr Kowalsky, is a notable pioneer in the use of sprayable vinyls for creating sculpture. His material is Cocoon, a sprayable vinyl plastic manufactured by the Hollingshead Corporation of Camden, New Jersey. This sprayable plastic solution is mixed with a special webbing agent and sprayed over wire armatures, constructions, and ready founds. Tough, flexible skins are created in this manner, and complex curvilinear planes are easily made. Working at relatively low pressures, the cocoon-webbing agent solution emerges from the orifice of the spray gun as delicate silken threads, which span the linear points of the armature and effect the formation of the sculptural planes.

Cocoon coatings were originally used after World War II for "mothballing" fleets of ships and aircraft. Today, the material is used primarily as an architectural coating. It is tough, weatherproof, and clings to most clean, dry surfaces to form a protective skin for buildings.

During a discussion with Kowalsky in his Paris studio, he outlined two basic operations which are necessary when this material is used for sculpture. In the first stage, the essential task is to form the curvilinear "skin" of the sculpture over an armature. Here, a combination of webbing agent (one part) is mixed with Cocoon (three parts) and blended for 8-10 minutes to attain the proper spraying consistency. This is then sprayed over the armature with a pressure of five to six pounds. A low spraying angle is used, and a cobweb-like skin is soon developed. The spraying is continued until a uniformly knit surface is achieved, and the required sculptural planes established.

In the second operation, the task is to build up thickness and to develop the final surface of the vinyl sculpture. In this stage, straight Cocoon is used, sprayed at 8-10 pounds pressure at right angles to the work. The Cocoon may also have a white flattening agent or pigments added to it to produce colored surface areas.

In Kowalsky's work, *It's for Today*, the sculptor has utilized wire armatures, department store manikins, and powerful electric lights within the surfaces of the sprayable vinyl plastic.

It should be noted that the chemicals used in this process are toxic and are potentially hazardous to use. Sprayable vinyls include such chemicals as acetone, methyl ethyl ketone, and toluene. Carelessly used, they may cause skin irritation, corrosive burns, respiratory problems, or olfactory fatigue. Very low flash points are involved in the use of these chemicals. The artist who is eager to explore this area should seek technical consultation with franchised representatives of the manufacturers of the materials, and should utilize strict safety precautions. Proper equipment and spray booths should also be used, as well as assistance from properly trained personnel.

**Vacuum Forming**

Vacuum forming is a process whereby a thermoplastic film or sheet is formed to the contours of a mold by the use of heat and a vacuum forming machine. The process involves the following steps:

(1) The artist makes a bas relief mold, which may be of either positive (convex) or negative (concave) design. Sculptural detail should be exaggerated to offset some loss of sharpness due to the thickness of the plastic sheeting. Molds can be made of plaster, wood, plastic, or metal. If plaster molds are employed, a higher density plaster should

be used, such as U. S. Gypsum's Hydrocal. The mold should be dry. No parting agents are required, but the artist should drill many $\frac{1}{16}''$ holes through the mold which will insure efficient conformation to the contours of the mold. These vacuum holes, or exhaust ports, are generally drilled in the lower relief areas of the mold. They serve the purpose of creating a uniform "draw" by effecting rapid air evacuation.

(2) The mold is placed on the table of the vacuum forming machine, and thermoplastic sheeting is clamped in position to a frame which is directly above the mold.

(3) A heater is swung into position over the vacuum table. In a calculated time period, the mechanism heats and softens the thermoplastic sheet.

(4) While the thermoplastic is hot and flexible, the frame holding the plastic is brought down over the mold and a vacuum is applied, exhausting the air from under the plastic sheet. Atmospheric pressure from above then forces the softened plastic sheeting against the mold.

(5) The vacuum is sustained until the plastic cools and holds its new shape. The form is then removed from the mold by using reverse air pressure, which forces the thermoformed plastic up from the mold.

Obviously, an artist is not likely to purchase a vacuum forming machine in order to create his work. Machines capable of doing large scale work are expensive. An artist may, however, create sculpture by this process. He need only create the plaster or wood mold in his studio and then job out the task of vacuum forming to a local plastics fabricator or electrical sign manufacturer. Smaller vacuum forming machines with table areas ranging from 7" x 7" to 18" x 18" are used by many craft centers and range in price from $300 to $1000. (See "Sources of Supplies.")

Typical thermoplastic sheeting and films used in vacuum forming are vinyl chloride, ABS plastics, cellulose acetate butyrate, acrylic, and polyethylene. There are a great number of other plastic films and sheets also available and manufactured in varying thicknesses. They are available in opaque, translucent or transparent colors, and metallized surfaces. Surface color may be applied by brush, spray, or silk screen either before or after vacuum forming the sheets.

Artists interested in light kinetics should be especially interested in this process; there are many possibilities for incorporating artificial light within thermoformed plastic sculpture. The process can be used to make architectural size bas reliefs and semi-flexible molds, which can then be used for subsequent lay-up or casting with liquid polyester or epoxy resins. If molds are to be made, be sure to use a thermoplastic sheet capable of resisting chemical attack.

Vacuum formed sculptures may be colored with a great variety of pigments and dyes, readily available from electrical sign manufacturers, or from suppliers listed in the back of this book.

**Thermoplastic Sheets for "Op" Effects**

The Edmund Scientific Company of Barrington, New Jersey, manufactures and distributes a variety of thermoplastic sheet which is suitable for experimentation with "op" effects. Many types of plastic sheet are available: translucent multi-lensed sheeting, transparent sheeting with printed moire patterns, plastic diffraction grating, and polarizing sheets. Exciting effects may be produced by placing one sheet over another to produce optical phenomena or to control colored light projections.

It has been my observation that most creative scientists and technicians are friendly people who have a kinship to art; they are quite willing to share their technical know-how with the creative artist. It is to the artist's advantage to make use of these resources.

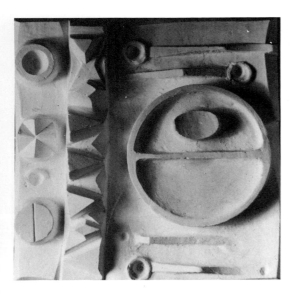

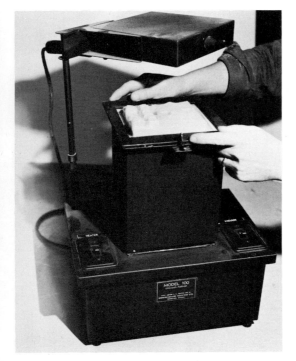

**Step 1:** (upper left) For vacuum forming, a bas-relief is carved from plaster of Paris. The panel shown here measures 6″ x 6″ x ½″ thick. Molds may be made of wood, metal, plastic, or other materials.

**Step 2:** (below left) The plaster of Paris carving is placed on the table of a vacuum former. Polyethylene sheeting is inserted in a holding frame directly over the mold and softened for approximately three minutes by the overhead strip heater. When the polyethylene sheet has sufficiently softened, it is brought down over the surface of the plaster mold and the vacuum is engaged. Heating time depends on the thickness of the plastic material. Generally, plastic sheeting sags slightly during heating before it has reached the optimum time for vacuum forming.

**Step 3:** (upper right) The vacuum formed plastic sheet is removed from the machine. Catalyzed polyester resin is mixed and poured into the polyethylene mold (the vacuum formed sheet). No release agent is necessary; castings pop out easily due to the flexible nature of the mold.

**Step 4:** (lower right) Here are the mold and casting in polyester. Architectural modules, sculptural components, and lamp clusters may be made of colored plastic by using these flexible, vacuum formed molds.

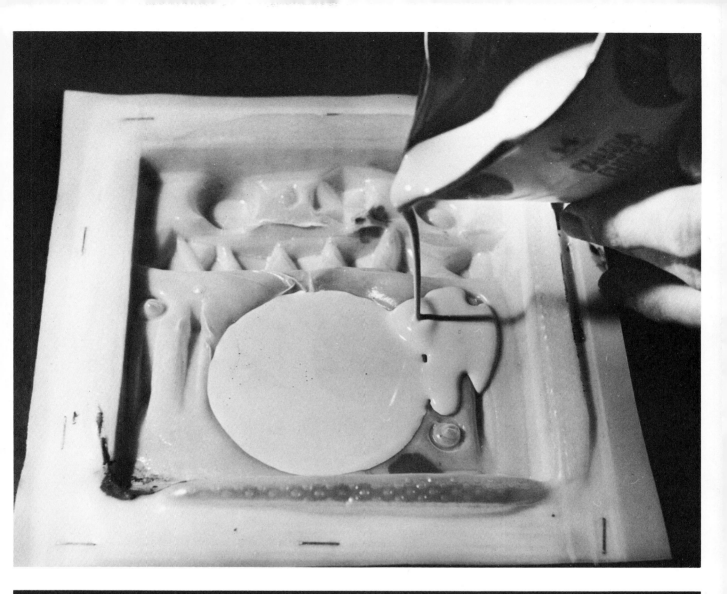

**Acceleration** by Yvaral, construction with vinyl cords. The cords are stretched in front of a pattern which is transformed as the viewer moves, seeing cords and pattern from a different angle.

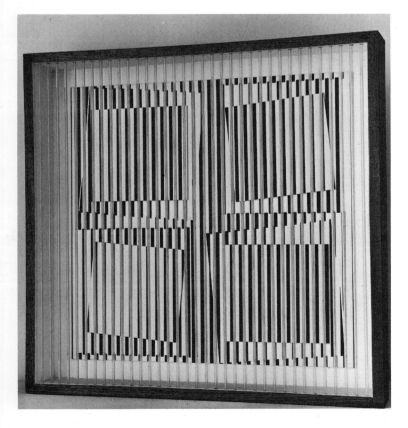

**Acceleration Optique** by Yvaral, construction with flexible vinyl cords. Spectator movement creates moiré effects and implied movement as the viewer sees the cords and background pattern from a different vantage point.

**2 Op, Circular Theme** (left) by Eugenio Degani, 150 x 150 x 25 cm., vacuum formed vinyl. This circular relief reflects the industrial origin of the vacuum forming process.

**Bird Form** (below) by Lew Carson, construction with acrylic. A flat, transparent acrylic sheet with a fluted surface texture is placed over a bas relief construction to produce prismatic effects.

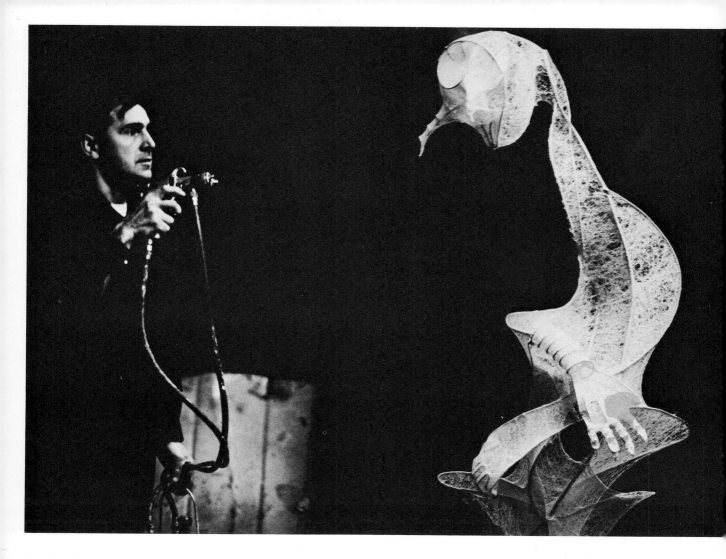

**Sprayable vinyl** (above) is applied over a wire armature. The silken plastic webbing agent spans linear points and forms intricate curvilinear planes and surfaces.

**Construction** (left) by Piotr Kowalsky, sprayable vinyl. A pigmented cocoon of plastic is sprayed over a welded wire armature.

**New People** (right) by William King, vinyl over aluminum tubing, courtesy Terry Dintenfass, Inc. Figures are first constructed of aluminum tubing; then the artist sews vinyl sheet over the metal armature. The largest figures are approximately 6′ high.

# Sources of Supplies

Note that some manufacturers may sell only in large quantities. Write them for the names of local distributors, or check the local classified telephone directory under Plastics or Boat Equipment and Supplies.

## Acrylic Sheet

Altuglas, 40 Avenue Kleber, Paris, France.

Cadillac Plastic, 148 Parkway, Kalamazoo, Michigan.

Cast Optics Corporation, 1966 S. Newman Street, Hackensack, New Jersey 07602.

Imperial Chemicals Industries, Ltd., Plastics Division, Welwyn Garden City, Herts, England (Perspex).

Plastic Sales, Inc., 863 Folsom Street, San Francisco, California.

Rohm and Haas Company, Independence Mall West, Philadelphia, Pennsylvania 19105 (Plexiglas).

Shinkolite, Mitsubishi Rayon Company, Ltd., No. 8, 2–Chome, Kyobashi, Chuo-ku, Tokyo, Japan.

## Acrylic Monomers

DuPont Company, Plastics Department, Wilmington, Delaware.

## Anti-static Solutions

Chemical Development Company, Danvers, Massachusetts (Anstac 2M).

Functional Products Division, Playtime Products, Inc., 442 N. Detroit Street, Warsaw, Indiana (Negastate 102 aerosol spray).

## Catalysts

Apogee Chemical, Inc., DeCarlo Avenue, Richmond, California.

McKesson & Robbins, Chemical Department, 155 East 44th Street, New York, New York 10017.

Wallace & Tiernan, Inc., Lucidol Division, 1740 Military Road, Buffalo, New York 14240.

## Cements (plastic)

Cadillac Plastic & Chemical Company, 15111 Second Avenue, Detroit, Michigan (Cements 1-B, 11, PS-18).

Schwartz Chemical Company, Inc., 50-01 Second Street, Long Island City, New York 11101 (Rez-N-Dye).

## Colorants for Plastics

American Hoechst Corporation, Carbic Color Division, Mountainside, New Jersey.

American Hoechst Corporation, Carbic Color Division, 129 Quidnick Street, Coventry, Rhode Island 02816.

Ferro Corporation, Color Division, Cleveland, Ohio 44105.

Patent Chemical, Inc., 335 McLean Blvd., Paterson, New Jersey.

Pfizer Company, Inc., 235 E. 42nd Street, New York, New York 10017.

Plastic Molders Supply Company, Inc., 75 S. Avenue, Fanwood, New Jersey.

Plastics Color, Division of Crompton & Knowles Corporation, 22 Commerce Street, Chatham, New Jersey 07928.

Ridgway Color and Chemical Company, 75 Front Street, Ridgway, Pennsylvania 15853.

## Concrete Plastic Additives

Dewey and Almy Chemical Division, W. R. Grace Company, Cambridge, Massachusetts.

## Disintegrated Metals (nickel, tin, aluminum, copper, bronze, lead, stainless steel)

Metals Disintegrating Corporation, P.O. Box 290, Elizabeth, New Jersey.

U. S. Bronze Powders, Inc., Route 202, Flemington, New Jersey 08822.

## Fibreglass Cloth

Burlington Glass Fabrics, 1450 Broadway, New York, New York 10018.

Ferro Corporation, Fibreglass Division, 200 Fibreglass Road, Nashville, Tennessee 37211.

Gustin-Bacon Manufacturing Company, 210 W. 10th Street, Kansas City, Missouri.

Pittsburgh Plate Glass Company, Fibreglass Division, One Gateway Center, Pittsburgh, Pennsylvania 15222.

Western Fibrous Glass Products, 739 Bryant Street, San Francisco, California.

### Fibreglass Laminating Equipment

Peterson Products, 1325 Old Country Road, Belmont, California.

### Fillers

Cabot Corporation, 125 High Street, Boston, Massachusetts (Cab-O-Sil).

Georgia Kaolin Company, 41 Parker Road, Elizabeth, New Jersey (clays).

National Gypsum Company, Buffalo, New York 14225 (limestone).

Plymouth Fibres Company, Inc., Traffic & Palmetto Streets, Brooklyn, New York 11227 (cotton flock).

Powhatan Mining Company, 6723 Windsor Mill Road, Baltimore, Maryland 21207 (asbestos).

Wood Flour, Inc., 3 Howard Street, Winchester, New Hampshire 03470.

### Gypsum Plasters

U. S. Gypsum Company, 300 West Adams Street, Chicago, Illinois (Hydrocal A-11, B-11, Hydrocal white, Hydrostone, Ultracal).

### Hot-wire Cutters

Dura-Tech Corporation, 1555 N. W. First Avenue, Boca Raton, Florida.

### Masking Compounds

Spraylat Corporation, 1 Park Avenue, New York, New York 10016 (Spraylat).

### Masking Papers

Permacel, U. S. Highway #1, New Brunswick, New Jersey (Permacel O1 pressure sensitive paper).

### Mold Releases

Axel Plastics, 41-14 29th Street, Long Island City, New York 11101.

Carlisle Chemical Works, Inc., 1801 West Street, Reading, Ohio 45215 (mold release waxes).

Dow Chemical Products Division, Midland, Mich.

Ellen Products Company, Inc., 131 S. Liberty Drive, Stony Point, New York (silicone mold releases).

Mitchell Rand Manufacturing Corporation, Hillburn, New York.

Specialty Products Corporation, 15 Exchange Place, Jersey City, New Jersey 07302.

### Molds

Devcon Corporation, Danvers, Massachusetts Urethane-rubber Flexane, liquid, putty).

Dow Chemical Company, Midland, Michigan (Silastic RTV).

General Fabricators, Van Nuys, California (Plastiflex).

Smooth-on-Manufacturing Company, 572 Communipaw Avenue, Jersey City, New Jersey (Smooth-on PMC-703).

U. S. Rubber Company, 1230 Sixth Avenue, New York, New York (mold materials).

### Multi-lensed Plastic Sheeting

Edmund Scientific Company, 101 E. Gloucester Pike, Barrington, New Jersey 08007 (op & moire).

### Ovens

Electric Hotpack Company, 5083 Cottman Street, Philadelphia, Pennsylvania 19135.

### Paints for Plastics (Industrial)

Glidden Acrylic Sign Finishes, Glidden Company, 11001 Madison Avenue, Cleveland, Ohio.

Keystone Refining Company, Inc., 4821-31 Garden Street, Philadelphia, Pennsylvania 19137 (Grip-Flex).

### Paints for Plastic (acrylic artists' colors)

Bocour Artists Colors, Inc., 552 West 52nd Street, New York, New York 10019.

California Products Corporation, New Masters Fine Arts Division, 169 Waverly Street, Cambridge, Massachusetts 02139.

Dana Colors, Inc., 1833 Egbert Avenue, San Francisco, California 94124.

M. Grumbacher, Inc., 460 West 34th Street, New York, New York 10001.

Morilla Company, Inc., 43-01 Street, Long Island City, New York 11101.

Permanent Pigments, Inc., 27000 Highland Avenue, Cincinnati, Ohio 45212.

Politec Company, Tigre 24, Mexico 12, D. F. or 425 14th Street, San Francisco, California 94103.

Reeves and Sons, Ltd., Lincoln Road, Enfield, Middlesex, England, or 16 Apex Road, Toronto, Canada.

George Rowney & Company, Ltd., 10/11 Percy Street, London, W1, England.

Shiva Artists Colors, Shiva-Rhodes Building, 10th and Monroe Streets, Paducah, Kentucky 42001.

F. Weber Company, 1220 Buttonwood Street, Philadelphia, Pennsylvania 19123.

### Plastic Sheets, Rods, Tubes

Commercial Plastics & Supply Corporation, 630 Broadway, New York, New York 10012.

### Plastic Impregnating Materials

Cal Resin, 14812 Raymer Street, Van Nuys, California (industrial coatings & resins).

Furane Plastics, 4516 Brazil Street, Los Angeles, California 90039 (Plaspreg).

### Plastic Molding Crystals

California Crafts Supply, Box 154, Buena Park, California.

### Plastic Film

Flex-o-Glass, Inc., 1100 N. Cicero Avenue, Chicago, Illinois 60651.

### Polyester and Epoxy Resins

Reichhold Chemicals, Inc., RCI Building, White Plains, New York.

Shell Chemical Company, Plastics & Resins Division, 110 West 51st Street, New York, New York 10020.

Taylor & Art, Inc., 1710 East 12th Street, Oakland, California 94606.

### Polystyrene Pellets

Shell Oil Company, Plastics Division, 110 West 51st Street, New York, New York 10020.

### Plastic Putties

Boyle-Midway Household Products, South Avenue and Hale Streets, Cranford, New Jersey (Plastic Wood).

Devcon Corporation, Danvers, Massachusetts (Plastic Steel).

Sculpmetal Company, 701 Investment Building, Pittsburgh, Pennsylvania 15222 (Sculpmetal).

Woodhill Chemical Company, 18731 Cranwood Parkway, P. O. Box 7183, Cleveland, Ohio 44128 (Duro-Plastic Aluminum, Liquid Steel, Gook).

### Plastic Polishes and Polishing Compounds

Costa Chemicals, Laguna Beach, California (Formula 5 Clean and Glaze Wax).

Goodison Manufacturing Company, Box 128, Rochester, Michigan (Triple A Buffing Compound).

Learock 765 for cutdown, Learock 884 for coloring, Learock 339 for high coloring; The Lea Manufacturing Company, 239 East Aurora Street, Waterbury, Connecticut 06720.

Mirror Bright Polish Company, Pasadena, California.

### Polystyrene

Sinclair-Koppers Company, Koppers Building, Pittsburgh, Pennsylvania 15219.

### Router Bits

American Rotary Tool Company, 44 Whitehall Street, New York, New York 10004.

Atrax Company, 240 Day Street, Newington, Connecticut 06111.

Edstrom-Carlson & Company, 1400 Railroad Avenue, Rockford, Illinois.

Oceana Tool Manufacturing Company, Inc., 4143 Glencoe Avenue, Venice, California.

### Routing Equipment

Delta Power Tool Division, Rockwell Manufacturing Company, 400 N. Lexington Avenue, Pittsburgh, Pennsylvania 15208.

Porter-Cable Machine Company, 700 Marcellus Street, Syracuse, New York 13204.

Stanley Electric Tools, Division of the Stanley Works, New Britain, Connecticut.

### Saw Blades (Carbide Tipped)

Forrest Manufacturing Company, 240 Highway 11, Rutherford, New Jersey.

Forrest Manufacturing Company, Inc., 231 Highway 17, Rutherford, New Jersey.

Lafayette Saw & Knife Company, 87 Guernsey, Brooklyn, New York 11222.

Lemmon & Snoap, 2618 Thornwood S. W., Grand Rapids, Michigan.

Radial Cutter Manufacturing Company, 831 Bond Street, Elizabeth, New Jersey.

**Saw Blades** (veneer)

Acme-Detroit Saw Corporation, 528 Fort Street, East Detroit, Michigan.

Atkins Saw Division, Borg-Warner Corporation, 402 S. Illinois Street, Indianapolis, Indiana.

Simonds Saw & Steel Company, Fitchburg, Massachusetts.

**Strip Heaters**

Electric Hotpack Company, Inc., 5083 Cottman Street, Philadelphia, Pennsylvania 19135.

**Urethane** (rigid)

Aircraft Specialties Company, Inc., 37 West John Street, Hicksville, New York.

Allied Chemical Company, Barrett Division, 40 Rector Street, New York, New York 10006.

Foam Division, Aircraft Specialties Company, Inc., 37 West John Street, Hicksville, N. Y. (expanded cellulose acetate, rigid cellular plastic).

Nopco Chemical Company, 60 Park Place, Newark, New Jersey (pour-in-place liquids).

The Upjohn Company, 555 Alaska Avenue, Torrance, California 90503.

**Vacuum Forming Machines**

Di-Acro Plastic Press, O'Neil-Irwin Mfg. Company, Lake City, Minnesota.

Spencer-Lemaire Industries, Ltd., Edmonton, Alberta, Canada.

**Vinyl** (sprayable)

R. M. Hollingshead Corporation, Camden, New Jersey (Cocoon).

# Bibliography

Cook, J. Gordon, *The Miracle of Plastics,* Dial Press, New York, 1964.

DeDani, A., *Glass Fiber Reinforced Plastics,* Interscience, New York, 1961.

Gutiérrez, José, and Roukes, Nicholas, *Painting with Acrylics,* Watson-Guptill, New York, 1965.

Lawrence, J. R., *Polyester Resins,* Reinhold, New York.

Lee, H., and Neville, K., *Epoxy Resins, Their Application and Technology,* McGraw-Hill, New York, 1957.

*Modern Plastics Encyclopedia,* McGraw-Hill, New York, 1967.

Moholy-Nagy, *Vision in Motion,* Paul Theobald, Chicago, 1947.

Newman, Thelma R., *Plastics As An Art Form,* Chilton, Philadelphia, 1964.

Oleesky, Samuel, and Mohr, Gilbert, *Handbook of Reinforced Plastics of the S.P.I.,* Reinhold, New York, 1964.

Percy, H. M., *New Materials in Sculpture,* Alex Tiranti, London, 1962.

Seuphor, Michel, *The Sculpture of This Century,* George Braziller, New York, 1960.

Simonds, Herbert R., and Church, James M., *Concise Guide to Plastics,* Reinhold, New York, 1963.

Society of Plastics Industry, *Plastics Engineering Handbook* (Third Edition), Reinhold, New York, 1960.